Working the Chesapeake

WATERMEN ON THE BAY

By Mark E. Jacoby

Lithograph drawings by
Neil Harpe

A Maryland Sea Grant Book
College Park, Maryland

Publication of this book is supported by a grant from The Chesapeake Bay Trust to the Maryland Sea Grant College Program. It is also supported by grant NA90AA-D-SG063 from the National Oceanic and Atmospheric Administration to Maryland Sea Grant.

Sea Grant wishes to thank the Maryland Waterman's Association for providing some of the photographs used in illustrating this book.

The opinions expressed in this book do not necessarily reflect those of the University of Maryland or of the National Sea Grant College Program.

Book design by Sandy Harpe.

University of Maryland Publication UM-SG-BK-91-01
Library of Congress Card Catalog Number: 90-071938
ISBN 0-943676-54-1 (cloth)
ISBN 0-943676-53-3 (paper)

Third printing with revised introduction
August 2000

For Jessie

CONTENTS

ACKNOWLEDGEMENTS

*W*orking the Chesapeake grew out of many trips I took with watermen as they worked their trade and harvested the Chesapeake's sea life. It was not always easy for them to share the small cockpits of their boats or the secrets of their work and lives, yet all were unfailingly gracious. My friends in the Maryland Sea Grant College communications group—Michael Fincham, Jack Greer, Sandy Harpe, and Merrill Leffler—were unsparingly generous of their time and insight, and everyone contributed uniquely to the completion of this book. Jill Perry Townsend accompanied me as artist and photographer on my trips around the Chesapeake, and though her work graces another effort, her talents infused and inspired this one. I don't see how I could have written this book without any one of these people and I thank them all.

Mark E. Jacoby

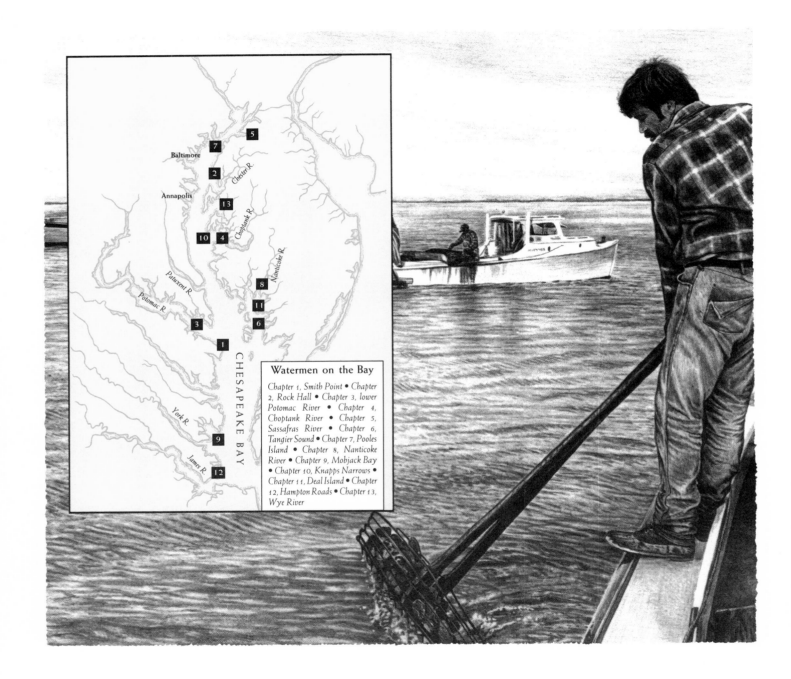

Watermen on the Bay

Chapter 1, Smith Point • Chapter
2, Rock Hall • Chapter 3, lower
Potomac River • Chapter 4,
Choptank River • Chapter 5,
Sassafras River • Chapter 6,
Tangier Sound • Chapter 7, Pooles
Island • Chapter 8, Nanticoke
River • Chapter 9, Mobjack Bay
• Chapter 10, Knapps Narrows •
Chapter 11, Deal Island • Chapter
12, Hampton Roads • Chapter 13,
Wye River

EDITOR'S INTRODUCTION

*F*or generations, the waters of the Chesapeake Bay have provided a home for independent fishermen. We call them watermen, and whether they are men or women, old or
young, the title earns them a certain respect in the region. Watermen often work alone or in
small groups, spending hours, days, years on the open water, far from the comforts of office or
home. Sometimes likened to frontiersmen who roamed the American West, they are in some
sense range rovers, living by their wits, and their range is the Chesapeake Bay.

One should be careful not to push the comparison too far—after all, watermen generally
descend from the very families that did *not* go west—but it is true that like the ranch hands,
trappers and buffalo hunters of the frontier, watermen have developed a rough wisdom, shaped
as their skin is shaped by wind and sun, ice and rain. No wonder that as modern life becomes
increasingly complicated we watch the Chesapeake's watermen with a wistful curiosity. Still
using the tools of their grandfathers, products of an old ingenuity, these watermen represent, in
some way, our cultural past.

To learn firsthand, from their own mouths and aboard their own boats, more about the lives
of Chesapeake watermen, Mark Jacoby went out with them in all seasons and in all weathers.
He followed Wadey Murphy in his pursuit of crabs, Ben Waters in his hunt for oysters. He
joined fishermen as they tended their pound nets, their fyke nets, their eel pots. Though his
initial purpose was to detail commercial fishing methods in the Chesapeake, he ultimately

shows us much more: the look of the water at dawn in a rising northeast wind, the sound of a waterman's voice—cast in accents from our Colonial past—as he speaks about his life, his problems, his prospects for the future. In short, through a style some might call impressionistic, *Working the Chesapeake* gives us the people and places that define the region's special character, not only the watermen's techniques but, in brief glimpses, their view of what may be a disappearing world.

As it happened, Mark Jacoby caught the Chesapeake in a moment of transition. When he first planned this project, Maryland's oyster harvest (to take one example) was holding steady at about two million bushels a year. Although nothing compared to the heyday of the last century, this harvest provided enough to sustain a long-standing fishery and the isolated Bayside communities that depended on oysters to round out their annual cycle of working the water. By the time the author had conducted his interviews and written his chapters (a long process since he covered every season and visited many watermen more than once), oyster harvests in Maryland had dropped to less than two million bushels, then less than one million, then less than half a million. According to the National Marine Fisheries Service, fishing effort—the time watermen spend in the pursuit of oysters—fell sharply from the beginning of the 1980s to the end of the decade. Far fewer watermen were seeking far fewer oysters. Without intending it, this book captures the rapid downturn—some might say the crash—of the Chesapeake oyster fishery.

Other changes were also taking place in the Chesapeake's fishing industry. The blue crab had become king of the commercial catch, surpassing oysters as the Bay's most lucrative harvest. During the 1980s watermen hauling in blue crabs saw a significant rise in profits, and during the 1990s the dockside value of the Bay's blue crab harvest averaged more than $50 million a year—and that's just fresh off the boat. Add multiplier effects for processing, retail and all the jobs associated with the crab industry, and that value climbs to more than $150 million a year.

Equally as dramatic as the blue crab's rise has been the fall and then the comeback of the Bay's striped bass. Generally known as rockfish in the Bay region, striped bass once filled tractor-trailers that traveled from ports like Rock Hall, Maryland, headed for Lexington Market in

Baltimore or Fulton Market in New York. Harvest figures for 1973 reached over 4 million pounds in Maryland alone, over 14 million pounds in the region. Those who gill netted stripers during cold winter harvests, when the fish returned to the Bay from the open Atlantic, hauled in healthy profits; but a precipitous decline in striped bass stocks, coupled with an appreciation of the Chesapeake's importance as the East Coast's major spawning ground, brought stiff restrictions and then a total ban on fishing for—or even possession of—striped bass in Maryland. Even before the moratorium, a drop in the striped bass harvest had taken an economic toll: one estimate put the losses of a diminished fishery in the Chesapeake at $24 million and 1,600 jobs.

Following the five-year moratorium, striped bass have come back, with populations reaching near record levels in the Bay. That fishery is carefully monitored and managed now, with harvest times and limits set annually, based on the strength of each year class. Because the moratorium was in effect during the making of this book, there is no description of the striped bass fishery here, only a description of the frustrations of some of the watermen at its demise.

In the background of these descriptions of Bay fisheries lie the workings and the transitions of the civilization that now makes its home in the mid-Atlantic. Though the focus here may fall on the quiet harbors of the Bay's water towns, the watermen make it clear that they feel the effects of development in the watershed and the subsequent decline in the clarity and productivity of their fishing grounds. At different points throughout the book Mark Jacoby reminds us, as he describes the ways of the watermen, that Bayside communities have suffered from rapid changes in the estuary. He alludes to the disappearance of underwater grasses and, especially in the book's final chapter, the great die-offs of oysters in waters starved for oxygen. Both these losses, he notes, scientists have attributed primarily to the overabundance of nutrients in the Bay, nutrients from septic tanks and waste treatment plants, from farm fields and suburban lawns, from the very air, now a conduit for nitrogen oxides spewed from ubiquitous exhaust pipes.

Though the ecological dynamics of the Chesapeake are complex, many declines in the Bay's food web and habitat unquestionably result from one essential cause: the rapid rise of population in the watershed. At the dawn of the twenty-first century more than 15 million people reside in this watershed, a drainage area formed from a network of rivers and streams which spreads—much like the branches of a tree—into the mountains of Virginia, West Virginia, Maryland and Pennsylvania, into the upper reaches of New York state. As scientists and citizens have made clear, those tributaries serve less like branches than roots, nourishing the Bay's rich estuarine mix—or poisoning it with toxic chemicals, sediment and too many nutrients.

It is no surprise that the watermen and the communities where they live feel a sense of anger and of loss. That anger is at times directed—as the conversations represented in this book reveal—at those charged with protecting and regulating the commercial fisheries, such as Maryland's Department of Natural Resources. The DNR and its marine police, as Mark Jacoby makes clear, had its beginnings in controversy during the bloody days of the oyster wars, and the agency often operates in the midst of controversy still. Whether from the mouths of former striped bass fishermen, highly regulated skipjack captains or oyster divers constrained by what they perceive as arbitrary restrictions, the testimonials of watermen seldom include kind words for the agencies that monitor and regulate them. One cannot help but think that much of their ire is aimed at the messenger who brings bad news. But also inherent in the indignation that sometimes rises from the watermen is a fundamental conflict between individual freedom and social responsibility—or, depending on point of view, social control. That balance refuses to be easily struck, and in the watermen we see the struggle most clearly. That struggle becomes still more poignant when one considers that the watermen themselves, in their very attempts at making a living, have at times stressed already weakened stocks of the fish and shellfish on which they depend.

For all these reasons, the future of the Chesapeake's water trades remains uncertain. Clearly towns such as Crisfield, on Maryland's Eastern Shore, no longer send trainloads of oysters cross-country to the restaurants of San Francisco as they once did. Change has without question stretched its inevitable hand to small communities like Rock Hall and Chesapeake Beach, where condominiums are becoming more common than seafood packing houses. But then some fisheries—like catfish—seem to hold fairly steady, while others—like croaker and spot—continue to rise and fall from decade to decade, drawing commercial fishermen and recreational anglers alike. Blue crabs come and go in great swings as well, and while they continue to bring a handsome profit to commercial watermen, heavy fishing pressure has raised concerns about the stock and has meant that crabbers have had to spend more time and money catching them. Meanwhile, the demand for Bayside restaurants and waterside facilities is growing with the expanding population, bringing a different kind of prosperity to the Bay region. Some seafood businesses are booming even if they have to bring in their seafood from as far away as the Pacific Northwest or the fishing grounds of Georges Bank or even the islands of Indonesia.

Whatever the future holds for Bay watermen, *Working the Chesapeake* has captured a moment in their history. Through carefully rendered interviews and astute observations Mark Jacoby has preserved for us a slice of life, a slice of time. His descriptions are embellished by the drawings of Neil Harpe, a well-known Chesapeake Bay artist who has a special interest in workboats and watermen. Formally trained and himself a teacher of drawing, Neil Harpe has made countless trips up and down the Chesapeake Bay to study and document the working fleet, some of which stands at the edge of extinction. The drawings reproduced here represent both a long standing affection and a disciplined attention to detail. The renditions of workboats and harvesting gear are as accurate as they are evocative.

One should note, too, that this book avoids the temptation of romanticizing or idealizing the watermen of the Chesapeake. The workboats reveal themselves as they really are, often driven by rusting engines without exhausts, riding low in the water, loud, filled on occasion with old cans, rotting rope and dead batteries. The descriptions of the boats and gear they use capture the watermen's ingenuity and their necessity. Old axles turn not wheels but spools for hauling dredges; a gear that pulls patent tongs from the water once served as the rear end of a Ford truck. Metal straps hold together splintered spars, and bilge pumps work overtime to keep afloat an old wooden hull.

Life is not easy in the water trades. But in these sketches of watermen it becomes clear that the life they lead is worth the price, and in some way their brand of freedom enriches all of us.

Jack Greer
Maryland Sea Grant

A PASSAGE TO PLENTY

Smith Point, Early May, 6:00 A.M.

Spectacular, this sight of fins breaking water, overwhelming in its plenitude. Tommy Williams, Virginia fisherman, watched as a power-driven dip net lifted fish from the pound net beside his boat, the *Robert Leo*. Moving easily with the rolling swell, Williams reached up and pulled the tie hanging from the dip net's lower end, releasing the catch as it came over the side into the *Robert Leo*'s dark hold. From net to hold fell a bright kinetic luminosity, a rapidly revolving kaleidoscope of silver that made, surprisingly, only the sound of polite clapping. The *Robert Leo*, filling with the weight of the catch, rode more steadily in the still-freshening southeast breeze. Coming into focus in the thin light were cow-nosed rays, blowfish, blue crabs, trout, bluefish, flounder, croaker, spot, sponge crabs, eel, and load upon load of shimmering menhaden.

"That's about the prettiest sight fishing I've seen," Williams said smiling.

He had arisen at 2:30 to arrive at his nets by 5:00, to be here fishing the Chesapeake's western shore for croaker, flounder, weakfish, spot, perch, the food fish that would pay his expenses and make his day, his season. In early spring Williams had worried stakes into the Bay's mud bottom in these open waters, just below Smith Point, the southern spit at the mouth of the Potomac River, boundary between Maryland and Virginia. He drove the stakes as his father had taught him, part of a family tradition, and in driving those stakes, Williams repeated an old lesson, learned in this region almost a century and a half before, a bit of Yankee ingenuity brought south from Long Island, where, some might say, the technique had worked too well.

The year was 1875, and it held little promise for a New England fisherman named George Snediker. Sensing the decline in local fortunes, feeling the pinch of his own constrained ambition, Snediker had decided to move on. He loaded his small schooner with food and clothing, with tools and cordage, with tarred cotton netting. He hoisted sails. Gravesend Bay, Long Island, dropped off his stern quarter, and under the press of a northerly wind on canvas he made way for Virginia.

Relative to New England, the Chesapeake region was then, as for much of its settled history, a southern backwater. Tidewater shores, lined with necks and creeks, with marshes and fasts, carried commerce reluctantly, and a plantation-style system of tobacco agriculture made for the settlement of widely spaced, self-contained manors tied more closely to England than to small neighboring towns. To New Englanders, whose shoreside cities were crowding, and whose harvests of seafood were perpetually faltering, the Chesapeake may have represented a kind of fisherman-developer's dream, a dream of large harvests and cheap labor, of quick riches.

First they came for oysters. By the dawn of the nineteenth century, New England oyster beds grew increasingly thin, then became exhausted. One by one, from north to south, New England oyster beds were fished out, then left behind. Massachusetts Bay and Wellfleet, Buzzards Bay and Narragansett, East River and Long Island Sound—all played out and abandoned, decimated beyond revival. Too many oysters had been taken with none left to replenish the beds.

That was the way Yankees fished two hundred years ago—catch as catch can, then move on. They moved on southward. The Chesapeake was shoaled over with oysters, Yankee captains had heard, was brimming full. They sailed south, returning with their schooners low in the water. They came first for small oysters, seed oysters, oysters they would lay on their depleted beds to mature. They came next for market-size oysters—the market was eager, the size flexible—finding greater profit in transporting large Chesapeake oysters than in growing out small ones. And they came now, Snediker among them, after the Civil War, for fish.

Snediker would have sailed on a broad reach for Cape Charles, then beat up the Chesapeake to Mobjack Bay, a four-fingered notch from the Chesapeake's western shore. Mobjack Bay was rimmed with pines and oaks and with farm fields beyond the woods. Its northern shore would be well protected from late winter winds, Snediker may have thought, and the closeness of the pines would ease his labor.

His labor centered on a novel piece of engineering. Taking long stakes of spruce pine, whole trees stripped of their branches, he hunched them down ten feet through the Bay's bottom. He started from shore, driving a stake every fathom as he went, until he had driven over a hundred. To anyone who may have asked, he would have called his row of stakes the leader. Working now round the leader's bayward end, he drove more stakes, perhaps twenty, in the shape of an arrowhead pointing toward deep water. This he called the heart. Bayward of the heart he drove yet more stakes, he built another heart, but with a flattened tip. This second heart he called the pound. And during the several weeks he spent driving his stakes, laying out his leader, his heart and pound, Snediker was not alone. Closely watching were farmers beyond the trees.

The farmers of Mobjack Bay were also fishermen, fishermen-farmers, and they had a proprietary concern for the clear green waters over which they carried their harvests. Using hand lines and shore nets, they fished the spring spawning runs, mainly for herring and shad, for their own needs and for the needs of their neighbors.

And when the runs were exhausted they put away their lines and nets for the year and turned to tend their chickens and sheep, and to till their fields. So with backward glances, in the early spring of 1875, they kept their eyes on George Snediker and his unusual engineering—they had never seen anything like it.

Pound nets were the most efficient fish-catching device ever to visit Chesapeake waters and they were here to stay.

From stake to stake Snediker strung a tarred cotton net, weighted at the bottom with chain. In the pound he laid netting along the bottom as well, forming, when he had sewn it together, a mesh bowl. What George Snediker had built was a fish trap, a pound net. As far as the farmers knew it was the first net of its kind in Mobjack Bay, perhaps the first in all the Chesapeake. Snediker caught trout and bluefish, flounder and alewives, mackerel and butterfish, sturgeon and "offal fish"—menhaden—and enough herring and shad, seemingly, to empty an ocean. And he caught them by waiting for the fish to come to him, to swim along the shore, up the leader, into the heart, into the pocket of the pound, where they circled until Snediker, in his own good time, arrived with a small net to dip them out.

Witnessing the tremendous volume of his catches, reflecting perhaps on the paucity of their own, the proprietary nature of the farmers' concern engaged fully, and found expression in the suggestion to George Snediker that there weren't enough fish in Mobjack Bay for his kind of fishing and theirs too, that he might want to consider pulling his stakes, setting his sails and moving on. Snediker ignored them—he was pleased with his catches and felt no itch to leave. By way of encouragement, several farmers sawed his stakes off at the water and took his netting to shore, warning Snediker that they would destroy his trap completely if he didn't soon quit Mobjack Bay.

Snediker came to see the persuasiveness of the farmers' entreaties and set sail for a friendlier encounter on the Chesapeake's Eastern Shore, but not before arranging the sale of his sawn stakes and netting, his leader, heart and pound, to a local farmer. When the farmer reconstructed the pound net, it too was destroyed. But the craft of its construction and the efficiency of its catch had been well learned. Within a year there were twelve pound nets on Mobjack Bay; within ten years there were forty-one. Pound nets spread up and down the Chesapeake, down to

Cape Henry, to Cape Charles, up the Rappahannock, the Potomac, clear up the freshwater reaches at the head of Chesapeake Bay. Pound nets were the most efficient fish-catching device ever to visit Chesapeake waters and they were here to stay.

More than a century later and fifty miles to the north, Tommy Williams, himself a descendant of the fisherman-farmers, now prepared to continue the tradition of working pound nets in the Chesapeake. It was 3:30 A.M. when he had put out of Cockrell Creek, stars still showing in the sky.

Cockrell Creek is a small finger of the Great Wicomico River, itself an unimposing tidewater stream draining the Northern Neck, a western shore peninsula bordered on the south by the Rappahannock River, on the north by the Potomac, by the Chesapeake on the east. Williams had set his pound nets, "traps" he called them, in the open Bay, just below the "hook of the point," the confluence of the Potomac River at Smith Point, an hour and a half's steaming from his pier at the head of Cockrell Creek. Because the market was slack and the competition was great, he intended to reach his traps at first light in the hope that he'd be first back to the buyer, and it was this hope that drove him from his bed at 2:30 this cool May morning.

Fifteen-knot southeasterly winds blew pungent and rank up Cockrell Creek, all the way to its head, to Williams's house and the pier beside it, where Williams leaned over the water pulling on the painter of a flat-bottomed skiff he would tie to the stern samson post of his fishing boat. He started the hemi-head Chrysler. He sprung the lines. Standing high on the raised deck, just aft of the low cabin, he motored slowly out the channel and into the foul breeze. Huddled together in the lee of the forward companionway were John and Hednum. Old and reticent, their black skin almost invisible in the darkness, they seemed indivisible from the creek, from the air. Following a course plotted in memory, Williams piloted around a treed shoulder of the creek. A factory emerged eerily from the darkness. Large and skeletal, with yellow lights suspended from high girders, belching smokestacks and cylindrical tanks, it resembled an oil refinery, which, in a sense, it was—the Zapata Haynie menhaden oil refinery faintly shrouded in yellow mist, there on Windmill Point, at Reedville.

Clear of the creek, the Great Wicomico River, and out on the main Bay, in continuing darkness Williams motored north toward his traps. With her round bottom and deep draft, her fore and aft cabins and midsection hold, the *Robert Leo* stood out among the Chesapeake's workboats, most of which have small forward cabins and V-shaped bottoms of little draft. "She's an old-time trap boat," Williams said over the throb of the Chrysler. "The oldest on the creek. Don't know if that makes you feel better or worse." Williams, young and blond, athletic looking in his visored cap and neatly trimmed mustache, was dressed in creased khaki trousers and shirt. He spoke slowly, deliberately, with a bit of southern drawl.

"It's not that bad out here. It's only every now and then you'll catch a big sea."

The *Robert Leo*, once his father's, was forty-five years old and had a penchant for rolling side to side in a crosswind. Crosswinds blew from the southeast, starboard abeam, and shoved along before them corrugated seas. "She's right sharp head-on and stern-to," Williams said as he leaned on the cabin to dodge the spray. "There's not a better boat out here—but side-on she rolls a bit. With half a load she rides ten times better." A large wave hit side-on and rolled the *Robert Leo* over a bit more than thirty degrees. Williams crouched low, both hands clenching the spoked wheel. "It's not that bad out here," he continued, smiling. "It's only every now and then you'll catch a big sea."

Most years he sets his stakes in February or March, depending on the weather, and draws them in November. His shallower trap has a long leader and requires two hundred and fifty stakes, the deeper trap about one hundred and eighty. He drives the stakes with a device he calls a "huncher," a sort of small pile driver. Williams and one or two crew take hold of its handle, lift it a few inches, and slam it down hard, thereby forcing a stake into the bottom. To drive the deeper stakes he'll often use a riding pole, a length of oak or gum chained crossways to the stake. Williams and his crew climb from the *Robert Leo*'s surging deck onto the riding pole and shake and worry the stake into the bottom. They hurry when they drive stakes—there's a rush to drive them as early as possible. The hope is to get all the stakes driven and the net set before the fish start running so as to catch the earliest runs and the most lucrative market.

"Nowadays it's usually between the first and the end of March we get the net out," Williams explained, "depending on whether you got good weather to get out and start driving, which you want to start doing by the middle of February. The last few years we have not gotten very good weather—you get out on the Bay one day, two days a week sometimes, driving poles, and that's all you're able to get. It seems like the last eight, ten years we haven't got as much good weather in the spring. I guess it was clean up to May before we fished some of these poles. I know that when my father was driving—he drove three stands—he could always get them in within two, three weeks. He'd start the last of February driving poles and usually by the middle of March he'd aim to have them in because the factory would start taking scraps about then."

Williams doesn't know when or by what means his forebears came to the Chesapeake, in pursuit of what fortune, by what coherence of events. That his mother's family sold the house he now lived in to his father's family in 1807 placed him in line with the fishermen-farmers. His grandfather had been a justice of the peace, a farmer, an occasional fisherman. Horses, cattle, sheep and chickens roamed his meadows and woods; in the spring he tilled his fields. It had been a farm much like the ones surrounding Mobjack Bay, fifty miles to the south. Increasingly, as it was handed down in pieces to siblings, the farm was less able to provide; increasingly, siblings grew dependent on the water.

According to Tommy Williams, his father was first on the creek to run traps all summer long—instead of only for the spring spawning runs. Running three traps made for very full days. "He'd use tarred cotton nets," Williams explained. "And he'd have to change parts of them every ten days. Two weeks is about all they'd last before they'd start fouling up. And just about every time he went to the Bay, he'd have to change a piece of net before he could fish. The amount of work he used to do was just really tremendous for what we do now."

The *Robert Leo* drifted up to the bayward side of the pound as a light rain began; the breeze freshened. John and Hednum set the *Robert Leo*'s lines, then muscled the flat skiff along the starboard side and jumped in. Hand over hand along the top-line of the nylon netting, they pulled their way over to the far side of the pound, to the part fed by the heart, while Williams chocked the pound's near side to the *Robert Leo*'s gunwale.

John and Hednum then pulled up the funneled entrance to the pound, sealing off the fish's only avenue of escape. Williams climbed down into the skiff, which by now had been worked around to the bow of the *Robert Leo*, and pushed it across the pound. Mesh by mesh, with considerable effort, the three men hauled the pound's net into the skiff. Rain and spray dappled their faces; sunlight danced on their slickers. Mesh by mesh they brought the skiff closer to the *Robert Leo* as they worked, until she was parallel and four feet abeam. In the pocket of the pound thus formed teemed a silver blur.

To have a profitable day, Tommy Williams must catch food fish, and these were mostly menhaden . . . the "offal fish" of the nineteenth century.

After the final load came aboard Tommy Williams lashed his dip net to the boom. The hull was half full, but Tommy's smile had fully receded. Today's catch, however tremendous its volume, was not a good one. Out of three thousand pounds of fish swung over the gunwale, no more than five hundred counted as food fish—croaker, trout, bluefish, flounder. To have a profitable day, Tommy Williams must catch food fish, and these were mostly menhaden.

Menhaden—the "offal fish" of the nineteenth century. Farmers dumped them by the millions on their fields, Reedville was founded on them, fortunes were made on them, and they remain this nation's largest single catch. But for Williams they don't fetch a very high price. For him and other Bay finfishermen, their most lucrative use is as crab bait, and if the buyer wasn't loaded up by the time he returned, Williams would sell them for that, receiving only three dollars per bushel, or six cents the pound. If he had to, if the local crab bait market was glutted, he would take his menhaden to the Huff and Puff cat food factory and receive three cents per pound. As a last resort he could sell them to Zapata Haynie for half that.

You can't make a full-time living menhaden fishing with pound nets in the Chesapeake Bay. Menhaden fishing now competes with large-scale agribusiness—soybean oil is a substitute for menhaden oil—and with South American anchovy fleets. Profitable menhaden fishing requires huge volumes, hundreds of thousands of bushels, such as are caught by the purse seiners of Zapata Haynie that fish the lower Chesapeake and the East Coast. The schools offshore are larger, the fish oilier. Both are needed to make money with menhaden.

Making a living for Tommy Williams means catching food fish, but like other Bay fishermen, he has difficulty finding them. For gill netters and haul seiners, for trawlers and purse seiners, food fish have become scarce. Over the last fifty years, and especially over the last ten, Baywide harvests of popular food fish have dropped precipitously. The harvests of herring and shad, striped bass and white perch have fallen as much as ninety percent. Some species have fallen so far they may not be able to recover.

The fish hardest hit are the anadromous fish—herring, striped bass and shad—the species that live in the sea but return to the rivers to spawn. The reasons for these declines are not clearly known and remain the subject of much speculative debate among scientists and resource managers, debate that centers on deteriorating water quality and the loss of habitat, on overfishing of these species in offshore waters and on overfishing in the Bay. Increasingly, their decline also appears to involve the housekeeping habits of an entire nation, of a civilization that uses the water and the air to dispose of its wastes.

Ironically, air pollution on the Bay has its cause not only in the Chesapeake watershed but in the Ohio River Valley. Tall midwestern smokestacks, made even taller to comply with the Clean Air Act, spew sulfur dioxides and nitrous oxides from as much as six hundred to over a thousand miles away. Eleven midwestern sources in particular, including one especially large power plant in Illinois, have been targeted as primary contributors to acid precipitation on the East Coast. Acidic emissions, when mixed with atmospheric moisture, become acid rain. And acid rain, as it suffuses through soils, leaches out aluminum, the equivalent of cyanide to newly emergent fish. The anadromous fish that run up the Bay to spawn leave their eggs far up rain-swollen creeks, in areas most affected by acidic runoff. The hatched larvae, delicate and developing, confront this bitter water and die off by the millions.

These may be deaths of a kind unprecedented in the Chesapeake, they may be the death rattle of an entire estuary, the nation's—perhaps the world's—most productive. Watermen—along with recreational fishermen—collude in these events by taking a declining number of brood fish, potential parents needed to replenish the stock, but they themselves may be indicators of a kind: by their presence, they reflect the health of the estuary; by their poor harvests and diminished numbers, they reflect a kind of systemic ecological malfunction, of which acid rain may be but one cause.

As the schools of fish have disappeared, the number of Bay watermen finfishing has fallen with them. Some leave the water, but many have moved on to other types of fishing, to oystering or crabbing, clamming or eeling—though some of these species are also threatened and in dwindling supply. Spend a day with a waterman as he fishes his nets or pots or oyster beds, spend a hundred with many, and a story would unfold about the Chesapeake and its decline, a story unlike that found in white papers or research articles, a story about the interactions of scarcity and plenitude—and the will of native peoples, the habits of a nation.

"Over the last ten years I've had maybe two, three fairly good years and the rest has been slack. It hasn't been enough to make up for the in-between."

Under full sun, motoring back in the daylight, the *Robert Leo* rode lower and flatter with half a load of fish in her hold. The wind had backed around to the southeast and smelled of salt. In the light, Cockrell Creek showed evidence of its decline. With the main fishery gone for the Gulf Coast, the shores showed only burned-out remnants of former factories, more prosperous times. "The menhaden fishery has gone downhill the last few years," Williams said. "Used to be eight to ten factories here, then down to two, and now just the one. This is the only plant on the East Coast. There are plenty of menhaden. It's just the price they're getting don't pay to catch them."

The *Robert Leo* was back on the creek by 7:30, early enough for Williams to sell his menhaden to the bait buyer. From the end of a long pier, a large stainless steel pipe lowered into the hold vacuumed the fish into a chiller, where they revolved on a Ferris wheel in a shower of brine, emerging clean and stiff onto a conveyor they slowly rode down the pier to waiting bushel baskets. The food fish were unloaded at the Reedville Seafood Company, lifted from the hold in a large steel basket hanging from a boom and dumped on a culling board, where the cullers, all black, separated them by size and species. Payment for them would be a few fish for dinner.

When he pulled up to his pier at 10:30 and cut his motor for the last time, Williams expressed ambivalence about the future of pound netting, doubts about its long-term prospects. "Over the last ten years I've had maybe two, three fairly good years and the rest has been slack," he said. "It hasn't been enough to make up for the in-between. I'm trying to hold a stance, keep my hand in it for right now, so I can go either way with it."

Like many another waterman after a disappointing day's effort, Williams was open to other lines of work. Like George Snediker, he was ready to move on. Several former pound netters on Cockrell Creek had switched to party boating, converted their boats from commercial fishing rigs to charter boats, complete with amenities for parties of recreational fisherman down for the day from Washington or Richmond, for which they may receive up to three hundred dollars a day—however many fish of whatever kind are caught. Williams thought he might try that. "Party boating," he said from the pier as he set the lines on the *Robert Leo*, "that'll be the next thing."

THE CYCLE OF THINGS

Near Rock Hall, Early June, 1:30 P.M.

"Now in the wintertime mostly I go clamming. Well, last couple of years I've been surveying for the state through Christmas. Then clamming, or whatever else."

"Huh—what?"

Chuckie Clark, skipper and owner of the workboat *Party Doll III*, was heading toward his eel pots. As he steered, he endeavored to explain the yearly cycle of his work as a commercial fisherman on the waters of the Chesapeake Bay, and Terry Potts—cousin-in-law, mate, needling editor—was having none of it:

"Pretty much from the fifteenth of September until the first of January you'll find him deer hunting," Terry said. "Yeah, he does a certain amount of deer hunting. If you don't believe me, just go on down and ask his wife."

Terry leaned far over the gunwale, trying to look Chuckie in the eye. "You told him you go clamming or oystering?" He turned back and took his pack of cigarettes from the engine cover, strolled along the cockpit for a moment as he lit one. Clam shells crunched under white rubber boots. Raising his right foot onto the washboard, leaning his right elbow on his knee, he addressed the water. "Yeah, he does a certain amount of deer hunting."

"Well, he didn't ask me what I did for recreation, now did he?" Chuckie stood in the very front of the cockpit, just behind the cabin and a cluster of levers that controlled the transmission and the *Party Doll*'s speed and direction. His cap proclaimed "I'm out for Trout," and his shirt, which sported an alligator, was tucked inside olive drab Grundens of Sweden Herkules double-bib overalls. Throwing the transmission lever into reverse, Clark emphatically gunned the six-cylinder Detroit diesel. As Terry grabbed a stanchion for support, the *Party Doll* shuddered and then abruptly slowed just inches away from a red and yellow buoy. Chuckie wielded a gaff into the water and hooked its warp. He wrapped it around a hydraulically operated flywheel, and pumped the pedal.

He paused to scan the horizon, then looked down at the water. "I don't do much rifle hunting," he went on.

Terry's eyes widened. He pulled on the bill of his cap, drew deep on his Camel Light. Smoke could have streamed from his ears. "Yeah he does. He goes to West Virginia, western Maryland. He goes . . ."

"Now, I said not much. You see, I eat them, but the wife, she don't like to fix them much and so . . ."

"She likes them alright, she just don't want to give him much excuse to go and hunt them. Course he don't need much excuse—"

The warp skidded out of the hydraulic wheel in a stream of water and splashed into a pile on the washboard. Chuckie smiled reluctantly, then broadly. "I don't do crab potting." He paused, waiting, but the assertion went uncontested. "Reason is, I don't like sea nettles and when you pot crabs you get a lot of them." Breaking through the water was an eel pot, a two-foot cylinder eight inches in diameter, made of hardware cloth, with funnels of double-knit polyester. Chuckie reached low for the pot, unwound the line from the flywheel and slid the whole along the washboard back to Terry.

In silence, for the first time, Terry untied the slip knot at the bottom of the pot and with a mechanical perfection born of long practice, dumped the contents into the live well. Eight small eels, one angry catfish. He pushed the expended bait through the pot and into the Bay, retied the slip knot, and shoved in two hands-full of horseshoe crab parts and three of partially

"I don't do crab potting. . . . Reason is, I don't like sea nettles and when you pot crabs you get a lot of them."

crushed razor clams. Along came another pot. Terry threw the freshly baited one over the side, advancing the line of buoys leapfrog fashion, one pot at a time. Time between pots: forty seconds.

～○

Chuckie and Terry had been at it since 4:00 in the morning, and it was now early afternoon. "Seems to me the earlier you start the earlier you get done," Chuckie offered up as rationale for the predawn hour when he first drove up to the gravel lot adjoining Cain's Wharf Seafood in Rock Hall. "Gets you back before the hot part of the day." The temperature now hovered around seventy degrees, a brief overnight pause in its climb to ninety-two, as light westerly winds blew into the harbor, bringing humid air. The foredawn sky was dark, showing only stratus clouds, thick and low, and a new moon. Summer had come to Rock Hall on the heels of winter, edging out spring.

Rock Hall lies low and quiet among farm fields and mixed woods of maple, oak and pine. Flanked by reed grasses, as well as low-rent commercial buildings and high-toned marinas, its harbor sits hard on the eastern bank of the Chesapeake Bay across from the Patapsco River and Baltimore, four-fifths up the Bay's length from the southern capes. Fishing—and increasingly yachting—are its main businesses now, but in the Colonial era its position between Philadelphia and Annapolis gave it passing prominence as a turnpike way station. Transportation was then a matter of mounting a horse and riding a short way to the next ferry, dismounting, sailing or poling or pulling to the far bank, mounting again and riding on to the next brook, creek, river or bay. George Washington, on accepting the surrender of Cornwallis at Yorktown, dispatched Tench Tilghman to spread the news to the Congress sitting in Philadelphia. The journey from Yorktown took seven days and was arduous in the extreme, particularly so the sail from Annapolis to Rock Hall—the waters were blacker than the sky, the captain uncertain of his bearings. Tench delivered himself to Philadelphia, to the steps of Thomas McKean, President of the Congress, where, rapping on the door at midnight, he was nearly arrested.

Washington himself traveled through Rock Hall often in his official capacity as first President of the United States. These events are recorded roadside along Main Street:

ROCK HALL, MARYLAND

FORMERLY KNOWN AS ROCK HALL
CROSS ROADS. MAIN STREET IS
PART OF FIRST ROAD CUT IN KENT
COUNTY IN 1675. GEORGE WASHINGTON
PASSED HERE EIGHT KNOWN
TIMES. TENCH TILGHMAN USED
THIS ROUTE FROM YORKTOWN TO
PHILADELPHIA IN OCTOBER 1781.

Philadelphians, joined by equal numbers from New Jersey and Delaware, have recently followed the same path. Bringing their yachts down to Rock Hall harbor for the summer gains them access to the broad protected waters of the northern Chesapeake Bay, from which they can sail to Annapolis, to Yorktown. In their foreign luxury cars they pass through town without pausing, past the St. John's Catholic Church (on Catholic Avenue), past the Rock Hall Methodist Church ("HOW VALUABLE ARE YOU TO GOD?") on their impatient way to their harborside summer homes, restaurants and marinas.

The historian Paul Wilstach would have failed to see the attraction. Taking his readers (in *Tidewater Maryland*) on a metaphorical tour of the Eastern Shore in the early years of this century, pausing here and there to recall "great plantations and eminent Colonials," he drifted "out of the Sassafras and down the Bay shore with a favoring ebb tide," to Rock Hall, of which he said, "The little harbor of Rock Hall is richer in memory of famous Colonial travelers than of ought else. Its day has passed."

Also past, for now, are the days of striped bass fishing, formerly Rock Hall's principal water business. Maryland had led the nation in the harvest of this prized food and game fish (also called striper or rock), and Rock Hall had led the state. After witnessing years of declining reproduction, and in loose federation with other coastal states, the Maryland Department of Natural Resources first banned fishing during the spring spawning runs, and then in 1985 shut down the fishery with a total moratorium. The striped bass fishermen of Rock Hall complained loudly, even while accepting compensatory surveying work from the state, but put aside their nets and moved on to clamming or crabbing. Some turned to eeling.

Chuckie and Terry had, before dawn, loaded the day's bait onto the aft deck. By 4:15 Chuckie had cranked up the big Detroit diesel, attached a floodlight to the aft edge of the plywood cockpit awning, sprung the lines and was now motoring into the harbor. Rain had been forecast and though it had yet to fall, the air held a ready fullness.

Terry stationed himself in a cone of light on the aft deck. A bait chopper—two coarsely beveled three-foot blades pitted with rust—hung from a pipe sleeved through the starboard washboard. Using the device like a paper cutter, Terry chopped live horseshoe crabs that had been plucked from the beaches of Delaware Bay. With quick guillotine-like motions, he chopped out small pieces that fell still writhing into a fifty-five-gallon plastic barrel, their tiny eggs coating the barrel and the cockpit sole with gray.

Chuckie was piloting from the cabin, heading west-northwest, out into the Bay. Beyond the harbor jetties the water picked up a noticeable chop, its spray peppering the windshield. The cabin, large and uncluttered, stayed dry. The *Party Doll* was airy and spacious, solid underfoot—and mortgaged to the bank. On the dash and overhead were a color CRT depth recorder, a VHF radio, a CB. Chuckie sat high in his chair, illuminated by the eerie glow of instruments.

"I started March twenty-third this year. I usually start last week in March. There's no season to it—starts when the water warms up. I go to November, Thanksgiving sometimes. About '77 or '78 they stopped striper fishing in the summertime. I'd already gone into eeling by then, but I'd stop when the striper fishing got good. Now it's eeling. I've done all right with it, but I would of done better with rock."

A light drizzle mixed with the spray on the windshield. Then the rains came, heavy drops illuminated by flashes of lightning. The sound of banging and pinging drowned out the roar of the motor. Terry stuck his head through the doorway. "I left my truck window open. Can we go back?" Chuckie turned around but Terry, not expecting an answer, was gone.

Ahead were the lights of Hart and Miller Islands, bulkheaded dredge spoil sites for Baltimore Harbor. Chuckie sent the shaft of a spotlight out to find the first buoy. He left his chair, donned his overalls and went to the steering station in the cockpit, where Terry was already waiting. The first pot came up empty.

And now, at 1:30, Chuckie and Terry were racing up a dotted line on the Chesapeake's surface, a wavy, meandering line studded with styrofoam buoys, red and yellow.

Almost squirming, a pot broke the surface, slithering with eels. Smiling, Chuckie hauled it up and slid it down the washboard. "Man, he's always on vacation," he said to no one in particular. "Didn't show up at all one day last week."

"I showed up."

"What time?"

"About one o'clock."

"Didn't know if he was a day early or a day late."

"Well now, you had to go and get started."

"Who started it? You started in about my gunnin'."

Terry upended the pot and emptied it into the live well, or so he thought—eighteen inches of writhing insinuation plopped onto the cockpit sole. He grabbed at it once, twice, three times without success. Grinning up at Chuckie, he said, "You want that eel? You want him? You catch him." The eel found a scupper and writhed into the Bay. "We'll catch him next time," Terry said.

⌒

The catching of eels dates as far back as fishing records go, at least to the Greeks, who preferred them smoked and considered them a delicacy, as many Europeans do now. Never much in favor with the American palate, the eels Chuckie and Terry catch are sent to Europe, live, aboard a jet reserved solely for their transport. Eels too small for the European market will be salted and used as crab bait.

Late in the last century, when shad and herring still made dramatic spawning runs up the Chesapeake Bay, the object of the Maryland eel harvest was simply the destruction of eels. Eels are omnivorous—they'll eat most anything, living or dead. What they seemed to prefer most, however, were shad, shad neither living nor dead but suspended between, suspended in gill nets. G. Brown Goode, writing of the natural history of aquatic animals in 1884 for the United States Commission of Fish and Fisheries (a forerunner of the National Marine Fisheries Service, NMFS), found the eel "a very undesirable inmate of rivers in which fish are taken by means of gill-nets, the destruction of shad and herring in the waters of the Susquehanna and others farther south being enormous." Goode's opinions were based on a general review of the Bay's fisheries by Marshall McDonald, also of the Commission, who recounted:

> Sitting in my boat while the oarsman was quietly rowing . . . we were attracted by a continual splashing in a net near by. We thought it to be a sturgeon rolling and entangling himself in the twine as they sometimes do. Heading the boat in the direction of the sound and coming near, it seemed at first to be a number of "herring" meshed in a singularly close huddle, and in their struggles flashing their white sides in the dim starlight. As we came nearer I turned the light of the lantern full upon

Never much in favor with the American palate, the eels Chuckie and Terry catch are sent to Europe, live, aboard a jet.

them and discovered a swarm of eels tearing and stripping the flesh from the bones of a shad which had gilled itself near the cork line. Gathered in a writhing mass, with their heads centered upon the fragment of the fish, we had before us the living model of a drowning Medusa. There was at least a bushel of them, greedily crowding each other, fastening their teeth in the flesh of the shad, and by a quick, muscular torsion snatching pieces from the dying fish.

By their voracious interference with gill netting, the eels were also snatching money from the pockets of Maryland's fishermen, fishermen who, then and now, didn't lack for clout in the

Maryland General Assembly. In 1888 the Assembly passed an act appropriating funds for the destruction of eels. Using oak-split eel pots —and one-fourth of its total budget—in 1892 and 1893, the State Fish Commission spent $3,413.25 in an effort to eradicate eels, to catch every last one, an effort that yielded, in public fishmarkets, $80.77. The report of the fisheries commissioners did not speculate on the effects of these efforts, but they must have been meager. Chuckie and Terry now catch five to six hundred pounds of eels on an average day, and the Bay hosts perhaps a dozen other fishermen like them. The annual Bay catch probably approaches a million pounds, although no one knows with any certainty—unlike most Bay fisheries, the harvesting of eels is completely unregulated. The people who collect harvest data in the Maryland portion of the Chesapeake, the Maryland Department of Natural Resources and NMFS, have no record of the number of eel pots Chuckie fishes or of his total annual harvest.

Forward lurch, reverse thrust, each punctuated with a roar and a belch of black smoke, forty seconds between pots—this was the pattern for catching eels. And when the pots started coming up empty, as they now did, Terry baited them and took them aft, where he stacked them for a later move. "Right now we're catching in deep water," Chuckie said. "We just move them around following where we catch them." The strategy seemed sound enough, except that suddenly the pots started coming up full, here at the same depth, eighteen feet, where they had been empty minutes before. "You got to learn to trick them," Chuckie said, shrugging his shoulders and smiling as he gaffed another pot.

All morning long and into the afternoon, the sun had been in and out of clouds, flirting with the thermometer, again hinting at rain. Suddenly it drifted behind a black anvil and seemed gone for good. Chuckie went into the cabin and put on his slicker, whereupon the sun reappeared with blazing intensity. "You see, it worked—put on my coat and the sun came out."

Full pots every forty seconds. Terry worked in unvarying repetition—full pot, empty pot, baited pot, ready for the toss with the arrival of the next. His bib and boots, his forearms, the cabin sole and the bait bucket, all had a fine layer of sequin-like gray eggs. There seemed no pattern to the catch, no reason to where the eels were, no consistency. Chuckie and Terry finished a row of pots and raced to a trotline, a single line of many pots and two buoys, attached at the ends. They lay this line in the shipping channel, where pots aren't allowed.

"Pots last anywhere from two to four years," Chuckie said. "But you'll lose them before they wear out if you fish them like drop pots. Here on this line you don't lose so many of them. But unless you're in one of these channels where the eels are bunched up, you got to spread your pots out to catch them. Can't use lines in the shallows."

Twenty-six individual pots, each with a four-foot warp, were held to the line with stainless steel hooks, which Chuckie removed as the line came through the flywheel. Some pots were of vinyl mesh rather than the usual hardware cloth and were slightly larger. "Them vinyl pots are the best catching pots I got," Chuckie said as one broke the surface in a roiling fury. "I don't know why that is. But you see that funnel? It's double-knit polyester. Water warms up and it stretches right out. I prefer poplin or gabardine myself." One by one, Terry took pots and stacked them aft. "This is just like the Army," he said, grabbing the last one. "Took them all up and now we got to put them right back overboard."

A yacht passed, forty-two feet of fiberglass, aluminum, Dacron—and smiles. Terry smiled back and returned their waves. "I don't think they're eeling for a living, the people on that yacht," he said. "Not likely." A large freighter on the final leg of a transatlantic delivery of imported cars (HOEGH-UGLAND AUTO LINERS) bore down on the *Party Doll* from the north. She had come through the Chesapeake and Delaware Canal and was heading toward Baltimore. "She'll turn when she hits them buoys," Chuckie said. "If she don't she'll be spending the night."

On to another row of drop pots. "We're doing better today than usual," Chuckie said as another came up full. "We just follow them to where the pots are catching at. It's just the cycle of things."

"State claims they don't migrate, but I know they do," Terry added.

"Some of them will bed down right here come winter," Chuckie continued. "The rest of them go on down the Bay and right out to the ocean. Them little ones are maybe one, two years old. They spawn in the Sargostic Sea."

The cycle of things for eels—their reproductive habits, their migrations—was a mystery much on the minds of naturalists and biologists from Aristotle on down, teasing the curiosity and knowledge of their observers. Aristotle thought they reproduced by rubbing together, that their eggs were to be found in the copious amounts of resulting slime, a view shared by Pliny and by other naturalists well up into the sixteenth century. That eels will envelope themselves in slime in response to any contact, whether from another eel or from a human hand seemed not to have borne on the issue. Later commentators, such as Leeuwenhoek and Linnaeus, seeing small wormy animals slithering in the abdomens of opened eels, believed eels viviparous, bearing their young live, based on the erroneous identification of intestinal worms as eel fry. Yet a third view of eel origins was held by many of the fishermen who caught them, as was relayed by the German biologist Jacoby in the nineteenth century:

> The last group of errors includes the various suppositions that Eels are born not from Eels, but from other fishes, and even from animals which do not belong at all to the class of fishes. Absurd as this supposition, which in fact was contradicted by Aristotle, may seem, it is found at the present day among the eel-catchers in many parts of the world.
>
> On the coast of Germany a fish related to the cod, *Zoarces viviparus*, which brings its young living into the world, owes to this circumstance its name *Aalmutter*, or Eel Mother, and similar names are found on the coast of Scandinavia.
>
> In the lagoon of Comacchio I have again convinced myself of the ineradicable belief among the fishermen that the Eel is born of other fishes; they point to special differences in color, and especially in the common mullet, *Mugil cephalus*, as the causes of variations in color and form among Eels. It is a very ancient belief, widely prevalent to the present day, that Eels pair with water-snakes. In Sardinia the fishermen cling to the belief that a certain beetle, the so-called water-beetle, *Dytiscus roeselii*, is the progenitor of Eels, and they therefore call this "Mother of Eels."

The "eel question," as it was often framed, occupied the best minds of continental biology. With many explanations and no definite proofs, a frustration borne of ignorance gave life to a range war of journal articles and symposia, fought with claims, counterclaims and refutations from biologists in Germany and Italy, France and the United States, over the discovery of ovaries and testes in adult eels. The battle was won with the undisputed discovery of male and female reproductive organs by Syrski, the director of the Museum of Natural History in Trieste.

Attention then turned to the search for newly hatched eels, in pursuit of which the Berliner Professor Virchow took the lead by publishing a notice in a fishery journal that found its way into the popular press; to wit,

> Hitherto, in spite of all efforts, science has not succeeded in discovering the secret of the reproduction of the Eel. The German Fischerei-Verein in Berlin offers a premium of fifty marks to the person who shall first find a gravid female which shall be sufficiently developed to enable Professor Virchow in Berlin to dissipate the doubts concerning the propagation of the Eel.

The good Professor, and his representative Herr Dallmer, the inspector of fisheries for Schleswig, were besieged by smelly packages and fantastic stories, stories of "great thick eggs," of eels live-birthed, of a Berlin eel seen to deliver twins. So great was the volume of correspondence that Herr Dallmer begged off his duties, leaving Professor Virchow to publish a notice excusing himself from receiving any more packages, having already received so many that he "would hardly know what to do with them."

For all the international claims and counterclaims, for all the public participation and popular press, the search for the eel's reproductive organs, for eel eggs, was nothing compared to later efforts to understand the actual mechanisms and geography of the eel's life cycle, a task assumed with single-minded determination by the Dane Johannes Schmidt.

It had been discovered by the Italians Grassi and Calandruccio in 1896 that a willow-leafed shaped fish called *Leptocephalus brevirostris* was actually the larval form of the European eel. And it had been known for centuries that eels migrated from rivers to the sea every autumn, and that while the migrating adults never returned, small finger-sized eels, called elvers, ascended fresh waters in the spring. The "eel question," as Schimidt framed it, was "whither have they wandered, these old eels, and whence have the elvers come?"

Setting out in the steamer *Thor*, Schmidt began surveying the Atlantic and Mediterranean for eel larvae, an effort interrupted several times by a shortage of funds (during which times

Schmidt appealed to His Royal Highness Prince Valdemar of Denmark for the use of merchant vessels) and by the Great War. Before he was finished, thousands of hauls by tens of vessels (merchant marine, naval and research) would have been taken between 1903 and 1922, the nets bringing up thousands of larvae of varying sizes.

There was a pattern in the sizes: the farther west Schmidt steamed, the smaller were the larvae. Their size dipped to a minimum in a region of the Atlantic south of Bermuda and east of Florida, called the Sargasso Sea, and then became larger again. Schmidt made cruises from America to Egypt, from Iceland to the Cape Verde Islands, through the Panama Canal, plotting as he went the size of eel larvae, constructing eventually a dartboard of oceanic scale with concentric rings of successively larger larvae emanating from a bull's eye in the Sargasso Sea. There were two overlapping bull's eyes, one for the American eel, and another, farther east, for the European. He concluded that the elvers that ascended European rivers in the spring had been three years in their travels, and that the American eels, distinguishable from their European counterparts by a slightly larger

Drifting with the Gulf Stream, the American eels ascend coastal rivers and bays, including the Chesapeake, in February or March.

number of vertebrae, had made their journey in one. Drifting with the Gulf Stream, the American eels ascend coastal rivers and bays, including the Chesapeake, in February or March, shortly before Chuckie starts setting his pots.

~

Chuckie paused in his race up the row. With four hundred and fifty pots fished and fifty yet to go, the buoy in the water was not his own. A foreign buoy, it belonged to Tommy Lednum, a Tilghman Islander who was potting his own bait. Terry gaffed the buoy and pulled it onto the washboard. From the barrel of chopped horseshoe crabs he withdrew four barbed tails and stuck them into the buoy. It resembled a satellite. "That'll give him something to think about," Terry said. "Something to see."

Forward lurch, reverse thrust. Forty pots left, the last row. "We'll get five, six hundred pounds today—two-fifty of the biggies, three-fifty of the bait," Chuckie said. "Get a dollar twenty the pound for the big ones, sixty cents the bait."

The big ones go to Europe, the small ones to Tilghman Island, to Annapolis, to wherever crab bait is needed. Yet they all squirmed together in the live well, wrapping around one another, forming one frothing, sliming ball of roiling eel. It was difficult to imagine how anyone could sort the eels—it would be easier to separate quartz from schist in a bucket of sand.

But Terry had a method. After the last pot was fished he aligned a sorting box the size of a small steamer trunk over a perforated barrel. The sorting box had a false floor made of slats separated by half-inch spaces, below which was a solid bottom opening to the barrel. The eels that could squirm through the slats, the bait eels, fell to the barrel below, leaving the large eels on top, to be returned to the live well, and then to a floating live car back at the slip, to a tanker truck, a Boeing 727 and, finally, Germany. Terry would then salt the bait eels. He would drag the perforated barrel aft, dip about a quart of salt from an eighty-pound bag (STERLING GRANULATED SALT), and sprinkle it over the eels. The eels would jump and dance, and then like vipers responding to an unseen flute, they would rise and sway. The barrel would froth. The alabaster opalescence, the shimmering white flanks, would dull to an opaque gray. Again Terry would sprinkle the salt; again the eels would dance, finishing, this time, motionless. Crusted now with salt and slime, the eels would be rinsed in the harbor and packed in blue-poly barrels (mushroom shipping containers from Shanghai) filled with a saturated salt solution, where they would keep for up to a year. Somewhere south a trotliner would use them long before that.

All this would come later in the cycle of things, after the last pot was fished. There would also be the buyer to meet, the fuel to get, the oil to change, appointments to keep with watermen come for their bait: pickled eels, eighty pounds the cask. Two young girls, dressed as ballerinas in the picture on the dash of the wheelhouse, would wait for their father's return. All that would come, but for now there were forty more pots to run.

PLACES YOU DREAM ABOUT

Bay Quarter Neck, Mid-June, 8:00 A.M.

An escalator burrowing along the bottom of the Potomac River made a circle of noise and smoke and water the color of coffee with cream, while up its eighty feet of stainless steel web track came fossil oyster shells, mutilated worms, and clams—broken and dismembered clams, cracked, belly-drooping clams, razor clams, jackknife clams and soft-shelled clams, the steamers of New England, *Mya arenaria.* Tucker Brown and his son-in-law Charles stood side by side, leaning over the starboard gunwale, near the noisy contraption that brought up all those clams. From its metal web they picked soft shells, whole and unmolested. "You have to watch it you don't get your finger in this web," Tucker said, pointing to sharp interstices that could easily capture a finger. "It'll take it clean off." It could also slice off the soft siphon of a clam, and as Tucker spoke many clams went by dismembered. Tucker and Charles eased whole soft shells into a plastic bucket at their feet as they worked, taking care not to break them. What they didn't pick off—what was broken, what they weren't fast enough to catch—arced from atop the escalator back into the river.

Tucker Brown lives by the river, by its banks, by its daily rhythms and long-term patterns. He refers to it simply as the River, and he refers to it often. "The thing about the river is your morning's always your better time," he said at 6:00 that morning as he motored out St. Patricks Creek, past St. Clements Bay and onto the river. The creek is small and sharply treed and redolent of honeysuckle. It may have first seen white faces three-and-a-half centuries ago, when, on nearby St. Clements Island, Maryland was founded by Papists with a yearning for religious toleration and the freedom to name their holdings St. Marys (now the name of the county and its largest city), St. Clements, St. Patricks. A half century before, the tidewater's first explorer and publicist, John Smith, had sailed up a Potomac "fed with many small rivers and springs, frequented by otters, beavers, martins and sables. Neither better fish, nor more variety for small fish had any of us ever seen in a place." Tucker lives on the creek with his wife and four daughters, next door to his brother, on land where his family has lived as far back as he knows of them. And as far back as he knows of them they have lived off the continuing abundance of the river, trapping its game, fishing its waters.

"Trouble is you got too many things coming due at one time. Too many people moving close to the water's edge, too many sewage treatment plants, too many chemicals washing off them farms."

Once on the river Tucker headed southeast toward Virginia, the far bank, his destination Bay Quarter Neck, a small bulge from the Virginia shore just above the Chesapeake Bay at Smith Point, fifteen miles from where Tommy Williams would probably be working his fish traps, dreaming, perhaps, of party boats. As a golden glare guided his course across flat water, Tucker steered from the small cabin of his workboat, the *Frisky*, which smelled of fresh coffee, a pot simmering daylong on the propane stove. Scattered about the dash were fossil shark's teeth, blackened and smoothed, dredged from the river bottom; the largest would fill a man's palm. As he piloted, Tucker spoke with some animation about the river, about his concern for its future. "Trouble is you got too many things coming due at one time. Too many people moving close to the water's edge, too many sewage treatment plants, too many chemicals washing off them farms. You got problems in your headwaters. Even if you stopped it now, you couldn't fix it in one year or five. Won't be like it was. I was eight years old when I put money in the bank from soft clamming. I ran ducking parties when I was fourteen. I used to trap muskrat, too. I guess I know this river and I'll tell you what, you'll never see stuff back in the river like it was no more."

As Tucker neared the Virginia shore, the Maryland bank disappeared under a low coverlet of white mist. Riverside Virginia was dotted with frame cottages set among hardwoods and pine. The navigating proved tricky, requiring a slalom-style weaving around dense thickets of stakes and nets. The trap fishermen were already at work, the ospreys and cormorants already waiting. White fishing boats with silver booms glinted in the early sun, their skiffs lost to view in the thickets. Nearer Bay Quarter Neck, the pound nets thinned, then gradually disappeared. Several boats of another sort had taken their place. Over their sides were slung hydraulic dredges, around which circles of brown water widened. They were clammers, among them the *Prospector*, her name in gold leaf on a transom brightly varnished, and the *Patricia Ann*.

Tucker circled around the *Patricia Ann*, backed to within hailing distance and shouted, "Catch any yet?" The answer drifted away in noise and smoke, but was finally landed on the third try. "The fella told me that if you hit a spot it's alright, but there's nothing if you don't," he explained. Tucker threw a lever that lowered the front of the escalator. Charles swung a six-inch-diameter pipe into the water, then started a deck-mounted Chevy V-8, which powered a pump that sucked water through the pipe and shot it out of jets on the escalator's forward end. The starboard engine in forward, the port in neutral, the *Frisky* moved imperceptibly ahead, scribing a circular wake, her dredge a maypole in the floor of the river.

~⌒

Now, at half past eight, four clammers slowly moved in tight circles on a mirrored surface to the droning hammer of hydraulic dredges. In their calm regularity, their constant rhythms, they suggested dancers in a grinding minuet. "We try to go in a straight line, like you would planting a field," Tucker explained. "But if the spot's small you got to go in circles."

You would not have seen them forty years ago, these oddly tilted, heavily laden craft. Unlike most Bay fisheries, clamming did not arise like a tap root from what Yankee Colonials or Indians had done. Chesapeake clam dredging arose from the mind of the one man who invented the device that would catch the clams.

The man was Fletcher Hanks, a Maryland native, who grew up during the Depression in Oxford, on the Eastern Shore. What Fletcher brought to his family during those difficult times was an enterprising spirit—and the desire and ability to catch clams. Whenever a northwest wind pushed water out of the Bay, accentuating the low tide, Fletcher would trudge out on Oxford's mud flats and look for siphon holes in the ooze. There he'd set his spade and dig for clams. He gathered clams for his family during the winter, when other foods were expensive and scarce; he gathered them for the boarding houses then clustered about the Oxford terminus of the Pennsylvania Railroad. Digging clams in this way was uncommon in the Bay, where people ordinarily didn't eat them, but it had been the tradition in New England since the time of the Colonials, since the times of the Indians. Unlike those found farther north, Bay clams were generally too deep for economical harvest, the tidal range too slight to expose much bottom. Fletcher's success in stocking the family larder gave him a mind to mine the Chesapeake's deeper ranges, to gather clams whatever the tide or wind.

A bright and self-confident man, Fletcher set about inventing a method for digging clams not from exposed flats, but from the submarine bottom of the Chesapeake Bay. Like many an inventor, he began simply, driven by instinct and elementary first principles, which manifested themselves in a bucket of sand and a garden hose.

Fletcher Hanks noticed that the hose would wash the clams up to the surface of the bucket, above the sand that had buried them, and reasoned the cause to be the respective densities of clams, water and sand. The density of the clams, being much closer to that of water than sand, allowed them to float clear of it. He took advantage of this principle in designing a manifold with nozzles that would shoot jets of water into the Bay's mucky bottom and dislodge the buried clams, and this he slung beneath a tractor. Behind his tractor he coupled a conveyor, with which he would cruise the mud flats in two, three, four feet of water. Bubbles would rise from the compressing muck; a widening circle of coffee with cream would spread from his tractor, and from the center of the gurgling light brown circle came clams. Dislodged by the nozzles of his jets, the clams floated up and landed on the conveyor, and were carried up to waiting hands and baskets. The system worked well enough to warrant refinement, which came in the form of a single, noisy contrivance Fletcher slung over the side of his boat, suspended from mast and boom. Through all this he carried on alone, working as welder and designer, thinker and tinkerer, inventor gone broke. In 1952, he perfected his device, sought out a patent (which he eventually lost) and started clamming.

As Charles worked, Tucker stood by the conveyor sipping his coffee, pleased with his growing harvest. There, in the cockpit of the *Frisky*, in his blue jeans and knit shirt, his tennis shoes and baseball cap, his Foster Grants, Tucker looked as well emplaced as a man could while working; he was a man in his element, a natural. Frustration attaches to any line of work, and clamming is no exception. But for Tucker, the frustrating aspects of the business—finding the clams, building and maintaining the rig—were at that moment buried in the deep past.

The dredge rig hung suspended fore and aft from three-inch horizontal steel pipes, themselves supported by stanchions bolted port and starboard to the bottom of the cockpit, the whole affair resembling goal posts. A hydraulic motor powered by the starboard engine turned a cog in the aft end of the dredge to rotate the webbed track, the Chevy's weight on deck, port side, helped balance the weight of the conveyor. Variously powered fore and aft, the escalator shook like a paint mixer—with pebbles in the paint. As would many Bay watermen, Tucker built his rig himself, both welder and tinkerer. "You have to be a jack-of-all-trades," he shouted as he turned back to the conveyor and picked out soft shells. "You have to learn how to work on your own equipment, whether it's a motor or what it is. If you run into a problem and can't solve it, then you have to pay somebody. You have to do your own welding. You have to be able to work and keep your own stuff going. You can't afford to go out and hire someone every time something breaks down." Tucker seemed well suited to this line of work, to fisherman-tinkerer; his boat was well kept and neatly painted. She could have been a charter boat, a party boat, a yachtsman's pride and joy—nowhere a rusty tool, nowhere a carelessly thrown clam.

The clams Tucker catches are destined for New England, the market opened by Fletcher Hanks, still the destination of ninety percent of Maryland's clam harvest. Hanks's early experiments with clam dredging soon had him hauling two hundred bushels of clams from each of several boats a day. As president and CEO of his fledgling clamming company, Hanks's roving presidential chair included within its range the helm of a clam boat and the cab of a tractor-

"You have to be a jack-of-all-trades. . . . You can't afford to go out and hire someone every time something breaks down."

trailer he drove once a week to New England. As the company expanded, so did the fleet of boats and trucks, until two tractors a day, five days a week, left the Eastern Shore and headed for New England. There were weekly trips to Louisiana and to Seattle, to every state interconnected by paved roads, except Montana and Wyoming, where coastal influences never intrude and beef reigns supreme.

Then change came like a mugging, unexpected and from a peculiar direction. According to Fletcher Hanks it came not from a scarcity of clams or a failure in the marketplace, but from the Maryland Department of Natural Resources. Under pressure from watermen's organizations, the DNR lowered the daily clam limit to forty bushels per boat per day and then fifteen, wiping out in the process Hanks's enthusiasm and his considerable investment. "Welfare for the watermen," Hanks now bitterly complains, "and the hell with efficient harvest."

"I got one rule on this boat," Tucker said as a fat clam slipped through Charles's already full hands. "If a good one goes overboard, you go over with it."

Tucker picked off rusty blackened clams from the conveyor. "Most times clams out of clay bottom will hold up better," he said. "Any dark clam is a good seller—they keep longer and don't break as easily. You'll catch right good clams here when there's any here to catch."

Tucker clams the Potomac River whenever he can, whenever the clams are there to catch. He likes to work near home—the days are shorter when he does, and he need not leave the *Frisky* unattended in a distant port. Often, though, he works the northern Chesapeake Bay. "You got problems in your headwaters," he said, offering his explanation for the frequent paucity of clams in the Potomac. But on this he may be wrong. Clams live in the Bay at the southern periphery of their natural range. Even in the best, the coolest, of years they live no farther south than the Rappahannock River, less than thirty miles south of where Tucker worked. That the Potomac is so close to this line of maximum southerly advance may account more than anything else for the irregular occurrence of clams there. And they are nothing if not irregular—one year they'll blossom into trillions of rice-sized clams seemingly sown into every hospitable clump of mud. And suddenly clammers are catching the daily limit by 9:00 A.M., as other watermen look enviously on, contemplating the intricacies of clam dredge construction. But the next year they may just as suddenly disappear, killed by heat stress, killed by the trillions.

Because of the delicacy of clams, their susceptibility to heat stress, their tendency to spoil quickly, Maryland has mandated that in the summer clammers must quit by 1:00 P.M. if they aren't equipped with on-board refrigeration, as none are. Market pressures intercede to enforce careful attention to spoilage, too—the buyers, both locally and in New England, quickly learn who is selling spoiled clams and the buying stops.

More and more quickly large blackened soft-shells rumbled out of the water up the dredge, and right on by. "I got one rule on this boat," Tucker said as a fat clam slipped through Charles's already full hands. "If a good one goes overboard, you go over with it." Charles raised his right foot to the washboard and readied to jump, though he kept his eyes and fingers on the web. "Yes indeed," Tucker said. "This is a good spot. With a spot like this it won't be too long till you catch your limit. I'd like to have it like this for two weeks and have the limit hold open."

Even more so than with most Bay fisheries, the limit for clammers is tied to what the buyers will take. The buyers place orders for as many as they'll accept, and when the clammers have harvested that amount they quit. "Whatever he tells you, that's what you go with," Tucker said. "The springtime of the year it's always slow until about the second week in June. From then till Labor Day most time it's just laid wide open. You don't even call the man, you just go ahead and get your fifteen everyday you can because you know he'll take them." Tucker pulled a hose-end sprayer that hung from his rig and rinsed his hands. "Course lots of times you can't get it," he said, sipping his coffee. "It's not like it was."

Tucker would enjoy his success, but doubted its relevance to a generally cleaner Potomac River. "I'll tell you what, you'll never see stuff back in the river like it was no more," he repeated. "Why my father, his father, and I don't know how far back, they was all full-time watermen. And you won't see it again like it was then. My father pound netted, trotlined for crabs and eels, haul seined, set some gill net, a few fyke nets, did a little turkling—all right here on this river. You won't see that no more."

Ironically, the Potomac could be called one of the few great success stories of environmental management, a modern-day environmentalist's dream come true. And the improvements have come so quickly—and run so counter to prevailing expectation—that many people, perhaps even Tucker, are unaware of them.

As far back as people lived along the river, the Potomac had been used as an avenue of transport, as a source of drinking water and food, and as a sewer. Early inhabitants' collective uses of the river were generally compatible because their numbers were low, their habits more mobile. Density makes a difference, and by the eighteenth century, the density of people on the banks of the Potomac River was beginning to make a palpable difference in the water. In Washington, D.C., the "sewer plant" consisted of pipes delivering raw sewage to the Potomac River and the city became known for its summertime stench. At the inauguration of Abraham Lincoln, the celebrants at the Capitol were rudely aware of the odor from the river. Water was drawn directly from the river, untreated, run through sinks and people and put back, to be drawn again. Typhus reigned, and claimed the lives of many—Lincoln's eleven-year-old son William among them.

By the 1950s the river's odor and foul scum caught the attention of state and federal officials. It being Washington, their concern first found expression in the form of a meeting. With three jurisdictions clustered around the Potomac River—the states of Maryland and Virginia, and the federal capital city of Washington—any action was sure to require meetings. Thus the Potomac Enforcement Conference, 1957, where they made recommendations. Fourteen years later, amid steadily worsening conditions, they held a second meeting. From this meeting came a Memorandum of Understanding that for the first time set specific goals for water quality requirements, measured by loadings of the nutrients nitrogen and phosphorus from sewage plants. For the first time, regulators would quantify and limit what went into the river as well as what came out, would attempt to take the privy out of the kitchen. In 1972, the Federal Water Pollution Control Act Amendments passed Congress, giving fresh impetus to restoring and maintaining water quality.

The goal was a fishable, swimmable Potomac River, and construction grants to the tune of one billion dollars would help bring it to pass. By 1975 chlorination of sewage plant effluents had reduced bacterial counts in the water, and the removal of phosphorus reduced the nutrient glut. By the time that billion dollars was spent, Washington's Blue Plains sewage treatment plant, the watershed's largest, had moved from primary treatment to advanced treatment; it had gone from dumping raw sewage to discharging an effluent nearly potable. The results were dramatic—sixty-eight percent less phosphorus, thirty percent less biological oxygen demand (a measure of how unrefined the effluents are). Water clarity went up forty-two percent, oxygen sixty-two percent. There were forty-four percent fewer noxious algae, seventy-five percent fewer bacteria, thirty percent less organic matter. But the real sum of all those numbers was that suddenly people were catching large-mouth bass from the center of the city, where a few years before they had held their noses and hoped for a catfish or carp. Washington's portion of the Potomac River had become fishable, and judging from the numbers of canoeists and kayakers, scullers and skiers, swimmable as well.

The goal was a fishable, swimmable Potomac River, and construction grants to the tune of one billion dollars would help bring it to pass.

At 9:30 A.M. Tucker shut off his pump motor and lifted the large siphon tube out of the water. He stopped the conveyor and actuated the lever that lifted it from the Potomac's floor. On his deck were thirteen bushels of clams caught in half a day's work. They would fetch over six hundred dollars from the buyer who would come to Tucker's cold room the next day. It had been an unusually successful day on the river, part of a larger pattern of emerging Potomac successes. But Tucker Brown would accept the day's catch as an isolated incident and not count too heavily on the Potomac's rejuvenation. He wouldn't celebrate the struggling return of a mighty river, only his own good fortune in finding a good strike of clams, a good place. "Those are the places you always hope you run across," he said from the cabin as he motored toward the Maryland shore. "Those are the places you dream about."

THE LAY OF IT

Tilghman Island, Early July, 5:30 A.M.

Wadey Murphy, his hand on a dip net, was talking about crabs. "They're funny," he said, eyes on the water as if they might be listening. "They're not like this other years. First part of the summer it was all Number Ones. Now that's good, but it ain't regular. Then they stopped biting. When they started again it was all trash. I don't know what's got them. Most times you got them figured out something else will happen. I tell you one thing. They can come overnight and you don't know where in the hell they came from. And they can leave overnight too. All I know about crabs is they swim and they bite. And that's all anybody knows about them neither." That, and that there is a rush on to catch them.

Up in the foothills of the Blue Ridge, across the Piedmont plateau, down to the coastal plain, all along the tidewater, the signs are everywhere. HOT STEAMED CRABS. From roadside stands, from restaurants, from waterside shanties, in the thick of urban activity and in rural outposts, hot steamed crabs are bought and sold and consumed by the dozen. Large white signs, roughly painted in block letters, crabs coarsely rendered in red—plywood billboards leaning against truck tires—images of crab hawking Maryland and Virginia style. # 1 JIMMIES. SHE-CRABS. CRABS—LIVE AND STEAMED. HOT SPICED CRABS. There is variety in the plethora of offerings but the main sellers are hot steamed crabs—live blue crabs boiled in vinegar or beer and water and liberally sprinkled with Old Bay seasoning. A man or woman, healthy and undistracted, can easily dispatch a couple of dozen and a pitcher of beer. In restaurants everywhere are newspaper-covered tables mounded high with crab scraps, with carapaces and claws, with gill filaments and swimmerets, in piles that may dwarf the diners before them. Open up the crab's apron and scrape aside the gills, take a finger and scoop out the white lump meat. Don't forget the claws—open with a mallet, a nutcracker, whatever it takes, takes, pull out the rich dark meat, dip in vinegar, perhaps some Old Bay, and eat. Follow with a hearty slug of National Premium ("Baltimore's Best") and reach for another crab, reddened by steam. Reach carelessly and you may be pricked by a spine that draws blood. Get a little Old Bay in there and feel the sting pierce like a needle. Have another National Premium and move on. Maybe an ear of corn, a rest for the fingers before the next blue crab.

Everyone is eating crabs and drinking beer. Norman Rockwell could not find a more familial-looking grouping of relatives united in singularity of purpose. It's a feeding frenzy. All around Baltimore and Annapolis, up on Washington's Capitol Hill, down on the Eastern Shore—in Ocean City, in Chincoteague, Wachapreague and Pungoteague, in Rehoboth and Lewes, in Salisbury and Easton and Cambridge, in Oxford and St. Michaels and Rock Hall, in Northern Neck and along the Potomac River, in Tilghman Island, even in Temperanceville, people are buying and eating crabs.

And in Tilghman Island they're also catching them. By trotline or pot, from the Choptank River or the open Bay, Tilghman Islanders are in a rush for crabs, and none more so than Wadey Murphy.

That morning, 5:00 A.M., Wadey Murphy was fueling up the *Miss Kim*, checking out the gossip at the general store, getting ready to catch crabs. "First part of the season we work creeks, say maybe for two to three weeks," he said as he topped off the tank. "Then the crabs start moving out. We spend part of May and June in creeks, the rest of the season out in the Choptank. We'll catch a few of them there in the Choptank alright." And with that he started the Olds, threw it in gear, and headed west out Knapps Narrows before turning toward Todds Point, about eight miles southeast, in the broad expanse of the lower Choptank.

The crabs had moved on out en masse—they must have; there were so many being sold—and the Chesapeake's crabbing fleet had moved out after them. From every tidewater creek, seemingly, some early-rising waterman was setting out for crabs. Potters with hundreds of pots each swarmed over the Chesapeake's surface, their pots dotting the water like apples bobbing in a barrel. Trotliners by the score laid out lines by the mile. Menhaden by the bushel, eels by the cask, bull lips and chicken necks, all for the catching of crabs.

The catching of crabs. Over the last fifty years it has exploded into the preeminent summertime fishery, for many watermen the most lucrative fishery of the year. Before that crabs were sought sporadically, and as often avoided. As late as the early part of this century crabs were taken mainly as bait-catch, or by-catch, as nuisance in the net. In New England they'd use them for cod bait, if they used them at all. And in the Chesapeake, they were as likely to be ignored as eaten. A shift in American taste changed all that. What had been by-catch became material for soups, soufflés, cakes and casseroles, for hot steamed crabs. The change was dramatic. In 1880, less than two million pounds of blue crabs were taken from Maryland's half of the Chesapeake; they had a value of forty-six thousand dollars. By the 1980s Maryland's annual harvest would routinely exceed forty million pounds with a dockside value of twenty-three million dollars.

"You'll find most crabs on the edges," Wadey explained as he slowed the Olds and readied to set his line. To do so he threw over a railcar brakeshoe, to which was attached a nylon cord that connected, some twenty feet later, to a blue-poly barrel and two plastic milk jugs all lashed together. Then came the line. From a large black plastic barrel, the trotline payed out over the stern as the *Miss Kim* crept forward. It skittered and jerked over its length, jerked over four-inch chunks of salted eel threaded through its braid every four feet. When the line was all payed out

Take a long line and tie a chunk of bait every three or four feet; tie it on directly, tie it to a snood; however you tie it, understand it's been done before—for a couple of thousand years at least.

Wadey grabbed it, gave it a couple of turns around the samson post, pulled it taut, and then threw over his other buoy, his other anchor. By the time he had finished, twenty-four hundred feet of line lay on the bottom of the Choptank.

The pressure was hot, the market was there, and Wadey was ready. But you can't rush the catching, not when you're trotlining crabs. Lay the line and wait. Drift, maybe check the news on the CB, see how others are doing. Whistle. Act nonchalant. Then you more or less sneak up to the end of the line first laid. Lift it gently onto a roller slung over the gunwale and go slowly forth. Trotlining for crabs is a rush in slow motion, practiced by a method little changed from the nineteenth century when fishermen first began intentionally harvesting crabs for sale. Little has changed, really, since fishing began. Take a long line and tie a chunk of bait every three or four feet; tie it on directly, tie it to a snood; however you tie it, understand it's been done before—for a couple of thousand years at least. If its fish you're after you can anchor the line and leave it. Once hooked, the fish will wait. Take them off when you will. With crabs its not so easy—there's no way to hook them so you work the line one way, give it a rest, and work it the other. You gaff it; you lay it over a roller; then crawl forward at slow idle, two, three knots at the most, and catch the crabs in a dip net as they drop off the line.

The first twelve baits were unattended. Then came the crabs. Up the line came Jimmies and sooks, Number Twos, Number Threes.

Wadey gaffed the line. He dropped it over his roller and grabbed his dip net. He hunched over and watched intently, dip net at the ready, poised for the swoop. He stared at the line where it parted the water. The first twelve baits were unattended. Then came the crabs.

Up the line came Jimmies and sooks, Number Twos, Number Threes. "Now your Twos are five to five-and-a-half inches and fat," Wadey explained as he dipped his net. The numbers designate male crab sizes in the scale of the marketplace. "Threes from five on up that are poor. The Number Ones, the Jimmies, they're the best—you'll get about sixty-five to a bushel. You get a hundred twenty for the Threes, eighty to ninety for the Twos. Most times a bushel of sooks—them's females—give you about a hundred; they'll pick out to about five pounds." He thrust his net and pulled it back, holding in its wire mesh six, eight crabs before he emptied it. Every so often a crab came near the surface, dropped off, and started swimming sideways for the blue beyond. But Wadey is world class—there is deftness in his stroke, rhythm in his motion. He jabbed the net deep in the water, into murkiness beyond his vision, and almost invariably came up with the crab. Once through he ran the line: seven Number Ones, six Number Twos, five Number Threes, and a bushel of sooks. The second run wasn't bad either, but on the third run the number of crabs dropped off precipitously, and toward the end there were no crabs at all. They just weren't there.

"I know one thing," Wadey said. "I thought the crabs would be inside but there ain't neither one here." Just then he scooped up a Number One Jimmy. "Hardly. . . . That was a terrible drop-off that time. I'm going to move to another place, I've not decided where. I thought it'd be better than this. But I'm satisfied to know how it is—won't have to worry about coming back." He flipped the line off the roller and motored toward the end of the line first laid.

Where the crabs went Wadey Murphy didn't know—but he would draw his line and reset it to find out. He gaffed the end, boated his anchor and buoys, and wrapped the line around a horizontally mounted, hydraulically driven flywheel much like the one Chuckie Clark and his fellow eelers use to draw pots. He stepped on the pedal and motored forward, drawing in the line as he went. Skitter, jerk, skitter jerk, fwap—it jerked clean off. "Aw shucks," Wadey said. He wrapped the line back onto the puller and started again, this time whistling forcibly. After about twenty yards, sensing no further trouble, he stopped whistling and started smiling.

"About five, six years ago a maintenance man from the packer retired and bought himself a trotline. But he had a bad heart and he couldn't get the line up. These pullers were originally made for crab pots. He went home and designed this here puller. After a few weeks he got it working good. When it first came out, I said, 'Shucks, this ain't no damn good.' But when he finally got her right, everybody got one. It's pretty good when the bait don't hang it up." The line sputtered in spirals down the inside of its large plastic barrel. Wadey hauled in the buoys, the anchor.

"I thought it'd be good inside but there ain't neither one here. I'll take her on up a bit." He opened up the throttle. The motor spit, and gurgled and clunked in response, sounding first like a washing machine, then like a drum corps. "It's this here flange that ain't right," explained Wadey. "She ain't lined up. Steering's off a bit, too—seems to be a hard spot in it somewhere." Seemed also to prefer circles to a straight line. Too obvious to warrant mention was the furious dribble exiting the water jacket of the wet exhaust. The automatic bilge pump groaned off and on in steady rhythm, counterpoint to the knocking of the off-center flange.

"I was about fifteen when I first started," Wadey said on the way back toward Tilghman Island. "Ninety-five percent of your crabs went to the picking houses back then. We put them in barrels. And every year there were more crab houses. I caught many a barrel at four cents a pound. That's a dollar sixty a bushel, but you couldn't make nothing that way. It's a bushel basket trade now. The only thing that saved the crab business was the bushel basket. You put them in a basket and sent them to the city. Used to be the only crabs you could sell in the city were great big Number Ones; everything else went into the barrels. Then in the 1960s the Number Ones didn't have to be as good. They were even taking Number Twos. Then even females found a market. It's the Orientals mainly that eats them."

Midway between Tilghman Island and Todds Point—near the mouth of the Choptank, one mile east of the open Bay, Wadey threw over his railcar brakeshoe and plastic buoys just west of buoy 61B, and payed out his line in the direction of Tilghman. "I'm going to lay in toward shore there, give me depths from eighteen down to ten so I can see where the crabs are." He laid her out and cruised her twice but there weren't many crabs and the reason seemed to elude him. At the end of the second run the CB cackled. Wadey's wife was on the air, making one of her daily radio checks, his connection with home. Wadey shared his unhappiness over the harvest and speculated on the reason:

"I think the good Lord is trying me."

"No, it's the devil that's trying you."

"Leastways there's no crabs."

The conversation ended with a promise of an afternoon hail. Wadey looked reflective, a bit uncertain. "There ain't nobody, especially a waterman, who lives by the wind, who gets up and sees things change as quick as they do, who doesn't believe," he said. "If he didn't, I'd think there's something wrong with his head. I ain't no holy-roller, but I believe. Every time I've worked a Sunday something happens—I'll break down. I don't believe it pays me, doesn't do me any good to work a Sunday."

He ran the line forward and back with continuing marginal returns. The crabs came up so infrequently that his rhythm was off when they did. One dropped off. He lunged. He missed. "Oh, you rascal," he said. While circling back for another run he talked about working the water, about his family's past, about its future:

"Now, my son trotlines in the summer. He's got his own little boat. I keep telling him there's no future in it. *I* wouldn't want to start all over again. He claims he don't want to be a waterman. And I hope he's true to it. Whenever it's blowing a gale I come up to him and say, 'Hey, you want to do this the rest of your life?' I'm trying to brainwash him now. I don't go to him on a good day. He's fourteen and he's as good as your average crabber. He's got his own thirty-foot boat. We rebuilt it. An old yacht, we cut her down and put decks on her. *Rip Tide*. He'll work his way through college, I hope he will. I'm trying to teach him the right way of things. I take him around and show him. I say, 'Look at this man—he got a new car, new boat, he's doing good.' And then I'll say, 'Look at that fella—no car, his boat half sunk. That fella's a doper.' My son, he knows right from wrong."

A crab potter passed, heading toward the main Bay, his canopy stacked high with baited pots. He, too, was looking for a better spot. "Now, they can't afford a bad day like I got here," Wadey said. "They handle a lot of money but they don't get to keep much of it, what with the cost of pots and all."

Wadey eased back the throttle and reached for his gaff. He stood by the roller as the *Miss Kim* drifted toward the buoys. He continued:

"My daddy was fishing over Parker's Creek on the other side of the Bay years ago, back when

"I think the good Lord is trying me."

"No, it's the devil that's trying you."

"Leastways there's no crabs."

pots first came on. They weren't legal over there. He was catching four to five barrels of great big Number One Jimmies and got a cent and a half for them. Then this guy comes up from Hooper's Island and says, 'You catch all those big crabs here? I'm going to set my pots.' My old man told him it'd be OK above or below him, but the guy went ahead and put his pots right where my daddy was working. My old man called the police. It weren't a year later my daddy broke down—battery went dead. And that same fella gave him a battery and told him just to bring it on back to Hooper's Island when he was through with it. I ain't got nothing against crab potters, no sir. They're regular people. But I don't want to be working by them. The main thing is they got a stronger bait to attract crabs so they won't come to the line. Plus, after they crab a

while they always lose some pots and then the trotliner's always in a damn hang. That's the lay of it."

Wadey gaffed the line and dropped it gently onto the roller. A raft of scoters floated off the starboard bow, their presence suggesting an early arrival of Autumn. Wadey plunged his net low in the water and missed the first crab.

"By rights, crab pots ain't allowed in Talbot County," he went on. "Period. Every now and then they try to get this area open to potting. But we outnumber them. You got to do it through the legislature and we outnumber them."

The catching was still irregular, with a heavy preponderance of the less desirable sooks. Wadey paused in his run up the line to separate a doubler, a pair of crabs, the female gently cradled within the skeletal framework of the downturned legs of the male. She soon would shed and be impregnated—soon would have; now she was destined for the soft crab market.

"One time the potters tried to get into Eastern Bay," Wadey said as he returned his net to the water. "Me and a friend of mine took petitions around to each one of those towns to stop the potters. I don't remember how many—maybe five, six hundred names on the petitions. We had this hearing. There were five or six potters. We had twenty-five testify against them. So we had them outnumbered five to one. The department wanted them to have more ground to kill off us trotliners. It seemed we had lost before it was started, more or less. Then this guy got up, all dressed up, and said, 'My name is Dudley Taylor, I am President of the Maryland Yacht Club Association and we think the crab potters have enough bottom now.'" Wadey lunged and missed and lunged again and caught a sook. He dumped her in the culling board, paused, smiled and said, "We never had any more trouble after that."

Wadey called it a day with eight and a half bushels in all, three Number Ones, three-quarter bushel each of Number Twos and Number Threes, and four bushels of sooks. He hauled his line and opened the throttle. The weather was fine, the winds east-northeast and moderate. The high wispy clouds and clear air, the thermometer reading of seventy degrees, all said October. The calendar said July. Wadey scanned the horizon with binoculars, as he had many times that

"I ain't got nothing against crab potters, no sir. The main thing is they got a stronger bait to attract crabs so they won't come to the line."

day. "It'd be a fine day for dredging," he said. "I love to go crabbing. I love to start, but when the season gets toward the end, I'm ready to quit. Same with oystering. I wouldn't want to do the same thing year round."

~

Wadey captains the skipjack *Rebecca T. Ruark*, one of the last of the Chesapeake's famed commercial sailing fleet, and the oldest boat still dredging. Built in 1886, she is more than twice the age of her captain. You'll not hear an "Aw shucks" or "You rascal" aboard the *Ruark*. If God overlooks the *Miss Kim*, it's the devil that guides the *Ruark*.

Wadey undergoes a metamorphosis sometime between the end of crabbing and the beginning of oystering. In winter he's a changed man. He stomps his deck, he barks orders, he curses the wind and the sky and the oysters and whatever falls within his peripheral vision. It's hard to imagine why, embracing that, he would spend his summers doing this; why doing this he would embrace that. But that's the way it is working the water—fishermen pace themselves to the rhythms of the work at hand. With trotlining they take it slow, meditatively slow because the crabs insist on it. Rush them and they'll drop off the line. The oysters aren't so particular. They'll lie there and wait, however boisterous one's efforts. And the faster the fisherman harvests, the harder he drives his boat, his crew, himself, the greater will be his catch, the faster he'll be to port. For Wadey, that's the lay of it, that's the way he works the water—and always has. On the water he is captain and master, president and CEO.

Not so back at the oyster shell landing at the Narrows, where shiny new trucks with large clean cabs brightly painted announced the presence of the buyer—BAY HUNDRED SEAFOOD, INC. CRABS, OYSTERS, McDANIELL, MD. More than anyone except Wadey himself, the buyer controls the amount of money Wadey takes home. Wadey does not like the lay of this. "Last three years I've been selling to the same guy. After three, four years they think they own you. After four, five years you got to get away from them. The job I dislike the most, this is," Wadey said, and one could see why. The market lies outside his peripheral vision: it ranges out far from his cabin and into the world beyond Tilghman Island and the Eastern Shore, out to roadside stands and elegant restaurants, to newspaper-covered tables piled high with hot steamed crabs.

A NUISANCE IN THE NET

Sassafras River, July, 8:00 A.M.

"Oweee! Damn water buzzards!"

On a tidewater tributary of the Chesapeake, in July, was a waterman who cared nothing for pursuing crabs, who would have just as soon seen them all washed away with the next ebb tide, who lay awake nights hoping the crabbers had caught the very last one. His name was Laws Hessey, and together with his daughter Pud he fished fyke nets and hoop pots in the Sassafras River for catfish.

"Damn. If I'd a known yesterday how bad the crabs would be today I wouldn't have slept last night."

The Sassafras flows into the Bay about twenty-five miles north of Rock Hall and just ten from the Bay's head at Havre de Grace. The Bay there is fresh to the taste the year round, the salinity never rising above three parts per thousand, a figure hospitable to catfish and crabs alike.

"These damn crabs'll drive you crazy."

Laws was fishing a fyke net as he cursed. A fyke net is a cylinder made of hoops and netting, with two funnels inside. The hoops are three or four feet in diameter and the cylinder may run twelve in length. It's attached to a leader, a length of netting that runs fifty yards from the cylinder to shore. The rig works much like a small pound net: fish swim along the shore to the leader, along the leader to the fyke net, and through the funnels to be trapped inside. Laws puts a couple of bushels of menhaden, "buggies" he calls them, or crushed clams along the leader so the fish don't lose their enthusiasm on that part of their journey. He also puts buggies or clams in the farthest chamber of the fyke net to draw the fish all the way back, except during the summer, when the bait also attracts crabs by the bushel. A fyke net without the leader he calls a caddypot, but he doesn't fish them in the summer because they are as attractive to crabs as they are to catfish.

"They'll just tear up the net is what they'll do. Nick up the fish, too. They've torn up leaders with holes I could've drove a boat through. Then you got to square them up and splice in a new piece. Goddamn waterbugs."

Laws and Pud cruise about twelve miles of the Sassafras in the *Hay Pud* to fish their nets. They leave port later than most watermen, 7:30, say, 8:00, Laws in the *Hay Pud*, live car in tow, Pud in a low-sided wooden skiff. They motor out a mile or so, anchor the *Hay Pud*, and set off together in the skiff. They'll come to a buoy in the water, a bleach bottle is common, an antifreeze bottle will do, and gaff the line that runs beneath it. Pud, working from the bow of the skiff, lifts the line over her head, and snakes it back a few feet. The tension on the line holds the skiff still in the tides and currents. Laws then lifts the line and chocks it into a two-by-four that sticks straight up about four feet from the gunwale opposite the net. He lifts the back of the net onto the near gunwale, glad when he does that the skiff is low-sided. He unties the chamber of the net and, using a dip net, scoops out catfish and mudshad and eels and crabs, mainly catfish. Sometimes a white perch or two will be in the chamber, sometimes a striped bass. The mud shad are invariably dead; he throws them into the river. There aren't enough white perch to justify finding a market, and the striped bass he's not allowed to keep; he throws them back in the river as well. The crabs he keeps.

It's not that he eats crabs ("Can't eat the damn things. Give me the gout."), or sells them—he's happy to give them away—it's just that he doesn't want them in the river. Would throw out every last one if he could. When other watermen are roving the length and breadth of the Chesapeake searching for crabs and appealing to the Almighty, when buyers are

When other watermen are roving the length and breadth of the Chesapeake searching for crabs . . . Laws is forever trying to give them away.

screaming for them and offering sixty dollars the bushel, Laws is forever trying to give them away. "Bad part is when you get home from the end of a long day and call up somebody and ask them if they want a bushel and they ask you if they're cooked. Damn things."

The catfish he also keeps. Live, large, healthy looking fish free from nicks he puts in a live well in the middle of the skiff. They writhe and squirm and flail about in a roiling boil of air and water pumped in by air-cooled motors set fore and aft on the skiff's plank bottom. These he takes back to the live car, a floating lath pen, where he keeps them until the buyer arrives with a tanker truck. Most of these fish will be transported to the Midwest, to Illinois and Indiana, from where farmers place orders to stock their ponds. Smaller fish, and those rubbed raw from the netting or gouged deep from crabs, he sells to a buyer for the "dead fish trade"; these fish go filleted to tidewater Virginia supermarkets. Real dead catfish, belly-up in the net, bloated and white, he throws over the side.

It's an unlikely looking composition here on the Sassafras, Laws and Pud, the *Hay Pud* and the live car, the skiff. The *Hay Pud* is a New England lobster-style boat minus the cabin. Laws bought her from a local marina that used her to ferry people and to tow boats. Laws uses her to ferry live cars and to tow the skiff; she is too high-sided to fish from. Pud, short for Pudding, her father's affectionate name for her when she was young, is young still, barely broaching thirty. She is tall and slender, graceful, quick to smile. Laws is heavy and lumbering and quick to giggle at whatever amuses Pud. The pair cruise up and down the Sassafras seated low in their gray wooden skiff, looking somewhat incongruous in their opulent surroundings.

"DOROTHY V," out of Philadelphia, "LADY JEAN," from New York, "QT5," from Lancaster, Pennsylvania—these are the yachts that lend opulence to the ambiance. As often as not, they or their brethren are to Laws just another nuisance in the net. "They're killing us. They run through the net. Average one or two every week. Nothing you can do about it. Why, this fella last week ran through my net and called the Marine Police—wanted *them* to do something about it. They did something alright—they wrote him a ticket and made him pay for my net." Laws giggled.

"ROHELDA," Wilmington, "MORNING STAR," Rosemont, Pennsylvania, "OUTRAGE," Norfolk, Virginia, "AZUNE," Annapolis. The Sassafras is inundated and overflowing with yachts, recreational boats in the parlance of regulatory officials, but yachts unmistakably. A quarter million a throw, many of them; their decks glow warm with Burmese teak, their fiberglass hulls glisten with gelcoat, their superstructures glint with polished chrome. Their curves are sensuous, their amenities luxurious. They tie up in rafts that would daunt the floating market cities of Shanghai, Canton. And they cruise up and down the Sassafras at speeds no less harmful than dangerous.

"There are too damn many of them," Laws said as a large sloop motored east nearby. A forty-foot Silverton ("LITTLE BUOY," Wilmington) roared by heading west, her Furamo radome and rail-mounted hibachi color coordinated in cotton canvas. She left a three-foot wake. The passengers smiled and waved. Laws waved back. "Saturdays in the summer we can't work because of them. Sometimes during the week, too. We got to go in, there are so many. They seem to settle down by five o'clock. I guess they're all drunk by then. We go back out in the evenings. Why some fella last week stopped the Marine Police and asked them how to get to Delaware Bay! And they's right here in this river!" (To get to Delaware Bay from the Sassafras: hang a right at the Bay, a right at the Elk River, and a right at the Chesapeake and Delaware Canal.)

Laws was fishing a net off a deep red cliff along the northern shore as he spoke. All his nets are along the northern shore; the water is deeper there, and the shore itself is owned in large parcels by persons benevolent and wealthy, "old money people," Laws called them, who don't mind the nets. The southern shore is dotted with cottages and gazebos and finger piers and boat traffic. The people there are perhaps not wealthy enough to afford benevolence.

As he tied back the chamber of his net Laws gazed downriver at a large cabin cruiser, the captain of which had for several minutes been attempting to set his anchor. "There's a real boater there," Laws said. "He puts the anchor one way while the wind's blowing the other."

Rolling hills and incised loaves of red soils border the Sassafras. The topography is unlike the Eastern Shore farther south, which is mostly flat, having hills that nowhere rise fifty feet above sea level, lower than some cliffs right beside this river. Laws grew up here, has fished and hunted here his whole life, rarely leaving the twelve-mile corridor of the Sassafras where he fishes his pots. He knows the area well. "There's locust, willow, beech, sycamore, honey locust, an ash here and there, red oak, white oak. Pretty much the same all over—lot of ash in places." He waved an arm as he spoke that took in its sweep the whole of the northern shore. He pointed northeast. "You know Black & Decker tools? Decker owns that there farm. Nice fella—you'd never think he had money."

His knowledge extends to the river as well. "We got a little bit of grass starting back in this river. First I've seen in ten years. Right round that bar and back into that hollow. We call it foxtail. We've had problems with fish, and that's the reason—no grass. There was just a little bit last year. And this year it's double that. Getting better. Wouldn't mind seeing other fish in this river again. I used to have five pound nets. Caught rock, herring, shad, mainly buggies. But help got hard to get, there ain't no more herring or shad, and you can't keep the rock."

The disappearance of grasses was the most visible of the alarming changes in the Bay that finally drew regional attention to the plight of the Chesapeake. By the 1970s, shad and herring had already ceased their voluminous springtime spawning runs up most of the Bay's freshwater tributaries, and the catches of other food fish, of stripers and white perch, and of oysters, were already showing dramatic declines. Many watermen, fearful of having their catches regulated further, or perhaps just hoping for the best, responded to these developments by saying that natural cycles were at work, pointing to previous declines in harvests, such as the great striped bass decline of the 1930s. The nearly Baywide loss of grasses (submerged aquatic vegetation, or SAV, as they are collectively referred to) seemed different, not so easily explained away. The

The disappearance of grasses was the most visible of the alarming changes in the Bay that finally drew regional attention to the plight of the Chesapeake.

suddenness and scale of the decline—from one hundred and fifty thousand acres in the early 1960s to less than forty thousand by 1978—seemed to suggest more than an individual species decline, seemed to suggest a deep systemic decay, a thoroughgoing ecological malfunction.

Bay grasses are food and habitat for overwintering waterfowl, and habitat and refuge for larval fish, for molting crabs, for settling clams, for a multitude of estuarine species, and their loss seemed to threaten a widening circle of other losses, like the expanding wake of a pebble thrown into a pond. Responding to popular concerns—largely focused by the congressional efforts of Charles "Mac" Mathias, then Maryland's senior senator—President Ford, in 1975, signed Public Law 94-116, one of whose provisions established the Environmental Protection Agency's Chesapeake Bay Program. In 1976 the Program began a seven-year, twenty-five-million-dollar effort to study the Chesapeake, to profile its changes, to find the causes for those changes, and to make recommendations for amelioration.

The loss of some grasses would invariably lead to a loss of more grasses, would invariably lead to acres of barren bottom, an underwater desert.

A major focus was the decline of grasses. Twenty-two scientists from the University of Maryland, the Virginia Institute of Marine Sciences, the Academy of Natural Sciences of Philadelphia, Salisbury State College, American University, Johns Hopkins University, the Environmental Protection Agency, the U.S. Fish and Wildlife Service, the Chesapeake Bay Foundation—an all-star cast of biologists of a kind never before assembled—engaged in a kind of ecological study that could only be called forensic. Four separate teams, each aided by a squadron of graduate students, surveyed the grasses, studied their ecological role, their susceptibility to herbicides and to changes in light. Twenty-two scientists variously working from nine institutions over seven years documented the loss of grasses and traced the cause to a loss of light—the Chesapeake was growing dark from excessive sedimentation, and especially from loadings of the nutrients nitrogen and phosphorus. The nutrients cause a proliferation of undesirable small and microscopic plants that float in the water and live on the grasses, blocking out the light. The Program's final report stressed that a reduction in nutrients was the only long-term solution to the loss of grasses and that restoration would not come quickly.

One could easily wonder whether restoration would come at all—so many were the sources of nutrients, so deeply rooted were they in the patterns of our lives. Nutrients enter the Bay from farm fields, from leaching fertilizers and animal wastes (grazing along the basin of the Chesapeake's mother waters, the Susquehanna, are more dairy cows per acre than anywhere else in the country). Nutrients also come from sewage treatment plants, many of which are only now being considered for the expensive upgrades required to improve them. And nutrients come from the Chesapeake's floating homes, the recreational boats, from country-club golf courses and backyard lawns, politically sacrosanct sources difficult to regulate.

Suspended sediments and nutrients caused a loss of light. A lack of light caused a loss of grasses. But the story didn't end there. Like a runaway feedback loop, the loss of grasses caused a further loss of light, which caused a further loss of grasses. Researchers for the Chesapeake Bay Program found that where grasses remained they baffled the waves and currents, thus preventing the resuspension of sediments that block light. Effectively, the grasses trapped the sediments and cleared the waters. The loss of some grasses would invariably lead to a loss of more grasses, would invariably lead to acres of barren bottom, an underwater desert.

In the Sassafras, meanwhile, the catfish had been as oblivious to the loss of light and grasses as had the crabs. There came a time when Laws would have to stop pound netting for food fish, but he didn't stop fishing—the catfish seemed to increase in proportion as the food fish dropped off. Catfish seemed to thrive in the darkened waters of the Sassafras River. The 1960 upper Bay catch, by Laws's father and a few others, was under a hundred thousand pounds; the 1980 harvest, by Laws and perhaps a dozen other fishermen, was four times that.

Laws hadn't read the Chesapeake Bay Program's final report, which would not have traced the loss of fish entirely to the loss of grasses—chemicals, acids principally, in the headwaters are probably more harmful. They drop from the skies during spring spawning runs and poison developing larvae. But Laws's observations on the return of grasses to the Sassafras were right on the mark. A happy anomaly of unknown significance (the flow of nutrients had not, after all, yet abated) had occurred, and, for whatever reason, the grasses of the upper Bay, which had been the first and most severely depleted, would, it now seemed, be the first to return. There was a twenty-six percent increase in acreage from 1984 to 1985.

By half past nine Laws and Pud had fished six of their twelve fyke nets and were coming to the seventh. "This one usually catches a lot of damn crabs," Laws said as he drew up the net, and, sure enough, as if on cue, three dozen crabs fidgeted and glistened in the bright sun.

Pud smiled and said, "Dad used to steam them up and this one fella kept saying, 'They're not hot enough. They're not hot enough.' Dad went out and got himself a big can of cayenne pepper. Those were hot enough."

"Damn if these crabs won't drive you crazy!" Laws said as one jumped clear of the net and into the bilge, where Pud scampered away before it. "Hell, they don't bite now," said Laws as he reached for the crab.

"Owee! Son of a bitch!"

"You told me they can't bite."

"Well, that son of a bitch can."

A fifty-foot Egg Harbor fly-bridge sportfisherman smoked past at thirty knots. Laws and Pud grabbed for the gunwales. "Oh man! And they don't realize the damage they're doing to that shore." The wake rolled up the red soil cliffs, and rolled up again; three times it rolled up the cliffs; three times the cliffs rolled back, dropping great chunks of soil into the receding water, pushing back the cliff, adding sediments to those already in suspension.

"They build a boat in New York and the first thing they do is bring it on down and drill a hole in the son of a bitch for a toilet," Laws went on as they watched the shore. "Gets like a cesspool in here." Unlike New York, which requires its boaters to discharge their toilets into holding tanks that can be pumped out at marinas, and which requires that boats not be fitted with through-hull fittings that allow discharge overboard, Maryland requires holding tank discharge in the Bay but allows overboard discharge offshore, where the effects are presumed to be less harmful. The result, naturally, is that boaters discharge their toilets over the side wherever they're sailing. One hundred and twenty thousand recreational boaters use Maryland's portion of the Bay, carrying as many toilets, probably, as the city of Annapolis, making for an unregulated contribution to the Bay's resources that fertilizes small plants that block the light—and that routinely closes marina-side oyster beds, which may harbor disease-causing bacteria.

Coming to the last fyke net, Laws was a happy man. He had an order for twenty-four hundred pounds of fish due Friday, needed to catch eight hundred today, and estimated he had about a thousand already. The last net was nearly full. "This damn fishing's got to be bred in you, I guess," he said as he dipped out the fish. "Otherwise you'd never do it. My mom, she fished—just like Pud. Took me in the boat when I was seven years old. Tied me to the boat she did."

On the way back to the live car Pud stowed away the dip net and tidied up the skiff. Laws totaled up his catch. "Now, let me see here, we got eleven hundred live and three hundred dead. And three bushels of those damn waterbugs."

A forty-two-foot Hatteras fly-bridge sportfisherman smoked off toward the west, coming within a few feet of a navigation marker, perched upon which were three osprey chicks, their parents absent. As the large rolling wake overtook their small gray skiff, Laws and Pud grabbed the gunwales and braced themselves for the splash, happy to be heading back to port.

PEELERS, RANK AND GREEN

Tangier Sound, Early August, 7:00 A.M.

Aboard the *Little Doll*. The wind blew lightly from the southeast, carrying the slight smell of salt from the open Bay, and of diesel exhaust from boats working nearby. A purple haze hung low on the Eastern Shore, and broken clouds grabbed at a red sun. Morris Marsh stood bent slightly backward at the waist in the open bilge and hauled a thick, wet nylon line. Hand over hand, slowly and with considerable effort, he pulled hard on a line that appeared to pull back. At the far end of the line was a double A-framed steel yoke behind which trailed a large net sock. When the yoke came alongside, Morris reached low for its eye, hauled it part way over the gunwale and high into the air. He leaned boatward and, with a slight wince, heaved it the rest of the way onto the washboard, leaving the bulging net bobbing in the light chop. He brought in the net a foot or two at a time, carefully shaking it out and folding it over the frame's lower bar as he went, like a bolt of fine cloth. When the net was mostly in he gave a final heave and slung its contents onto the washboard.

What spilled from the net was grass—eelgrass and widgeon grass and horned pondweed, neatly rolled like carpet. The eelgrass, resembling Kentucky Blue, feathered finely into tight swirls like birds' nests. In the swirls were shrimp and pipefish, minnows and hogchokers, flounders and croakers, and hard crabs, Number One Jimmies and sooks. They lacked ferocity, these nested crabs; they would not have offended even Laws Hessey. Tightly trussed about their limbs by the rolled grass, they were held defenseless. Morris pulled away the grass and tossed the hard crabs unceremoniously into a bushel basket on the aft deck. He paid little notice to their size and sex and did not measure them. What he was after were molting crabs and crabs ready to molt—peelers, rank and green, busters, and soft crabs ready made.

~~~

The shell of a blue crab is inelastic and hard; it can't expand like skin, can't grow along its margin like a clam shell. Once formed it is unmalleable, fixed and unchangeable. Technically speaking, it's not a shell at all, but a carapace, a dense horny matrix of proteins and calcium and chitin, chemicals secreted by the developing crab that align and interlock to form the organic equivalent of plastic. It's an effective covering—hard crabs have few predators—but like a new baby's plastic bracelet it grows small in proportion as the crab grows larger. A point is reached when, if it's to continue growing, if it's to avoid becoming entombed in its own exoskeleton, the crab must cast off its confining shell and escape to form a new one.

The escape, called molting or ecdysis by biologists and shedding or peeling by Bay watermen, occurs every few days during the crab's fast-growing first year, and then with decreasing frequency throughout its life. The process is difficult—the crab must withdraw from its carapace eight multi-jointed spindly appendages as well as its irregularly fusiform body, and is often unsuccessful in doing so.

Even when the crab succeeds in molting, when it doesn't "hang up," its difficulties are not over—it emerges from its shell soft and limp, powerless to feed or to fend off predators, vulnerable to virtually anything that crawls or swims. To protect itself, the crab, following some presentient internal signal of its forthcoming molt, searches out a safe place to hide.

Scattered throughout the Bay are many desirable places, such as a hollow submarine log, or an empty bomb casing. The best place, though, a veritable soft crab haven, is a lush meadow of underwater grasses. There, the crab may scutter down to the roots to await its transformation in some security.

Though greatly diminished relative to times past, the Chesapeake has many such meadows. The largest and lushest carpets the bottom of Tangier Sound, a shallow arm of the Maryland's southern Bay. Protected from the scouring effect of the Bay's main current by a string of islands that curve south from the Dorchester marshes, the shallows of Tangier Sound are home to more grasses and more soft crabs than anywhere else in the Bay, probably in the world. Crabs come here in huge numbers to shed, inaccessible in the eelgrass to bluefish or sea trout. Other crabs can't find them, nor can eels or turtles, gulls or herons. The shedders are secure from nearly anything that would find them, and their security might well be complete, except for Morris Marsh.

Morris had gotten up at 3:30 A.M., left the dock at 4:00. He motored the *Little Doll* out a narrow swale along the banks of Ewell, Smith Island, the spire of the Methodist Church behind him aglow in artifical light.

Smith Island is three hundred acres of sand ridge and marsh, thoroughfare and hummock, forty-five minutes by fast cruiser from the Eastern Shore. Together with Tangier Island, South Marsh, Holland and Bloodsworth islands, Smith Island forms the western rim to Tangier Sound. Its history is obscure and often confounded with the Smith Island on the Atlantic side of Cape Charles, at the tip of the Eastern Shore, which was first visited in 1608 by John Smith, who was seeking a site for a saltworks. The Smith Island of Tangier Sound was probably one of the Isles of Limbo, so named by Smith because there his party encountered "the wind and waters so much increased, with thunder, lightning and rain, that our foremast blew overboard, and such mighty waves overwrought us in that small barge, that with great labor, we kept her from sinking by freeing out the water. Two days were we enforced to inhabit these uninhabited isles; which, for the exception of gusts, thunder, rain, storms and ill weather, we called Limbo." In the seventeenth and eighteenth centuries the Isles of Limbo were likely used for cattle grazing—many lower Eastern Shore islands were bought by English overlords and used for that purpose. Gradually, one of the islands came to be called Smith, and came to be settled by hardy individualists who farmed its sandy soil, trudged through its marshes for turtles and crabs and fished its surrounding waters for stripers and perch, spot and croaker. Between six and seven hundred people, many a Marsh among them, live there now in the towns of Rhodes Point, Tylerton and Ewell.

Morris threaded his way in darkness, Ewell's spire behind him, through Smith Island's northern marshes to the open Bay, the *Little Doll*'s wake sparkling in the moonlight as it rolled through the grasses.

"We're heading for the big dipper," he said. "'Keep her on the dipper,' that's what my daddy used to say." Morris spoke thickly, his vowels deep and long, his rhythm sing-song up to the penultimate word, which was longest and highest in tone and which he followed with a slight inflection. The accents of Smith Island, long kept pure in their isolation, are often described as Elizabethan.

By 5:00 A.M., glowing layers of pink and purple softened the eastern horizon. Off to starboard were the marker beacons of Fog's Point and Kedges Straits, low stars on a black sea. Morris piloted the *Little Doll* north on the slight swells of the open Bay.

Morris had been crabbing for thirty years, always from early May until the the first week of October.

Morris had been crabbing for thirty years, always from early May until the the first week of October. "I believe I do like crabbing more than oystering," he said over the throb of the diesel. One reason is that for several years prior to the last two he had had to leave the island for weeks at a time to oyster in more northerly waters because MSX, an oyster parasite, had decimated the local beds. The situation seemed a little better now, though the recurring pattern of the disease's infestation, which erupts and spreads when a lack of rainfall increases the Bay's salinity, made it likely he would have to leave again.

For his winter work and travels, Morris owns a boat much larger than the one he uses for crabbing, a vessel properly fitted with a spacious cabin and all the amenities, including TV, stereo, stove, heater, "everything." Aboard Chesapeake Bay workboats, "everything" also means a bucket for a toilet.

Morris's crabbing boat is without those amenities. Of a model called a Jenkin's Creeker, after the mainland creek where many were built, it is finely shaped, simply made, and beautiful, its lines dramatic—the sheer sweeps up grandly toward the bow from a stern low enough to appear unseaworthy, the freeboard there less than eighteen inches. Its bottom is a shallow V, wide for its length—ten feet wide and only thirty long. It has no cabin, its only enclosure a plywood motor box resting prominently high in the midsection. Originally Jenkin's Creekers were sailing boats, and Morris's was little changed from the original lines—it appeared you could take out the engine, install a centerboard in its place, step a mast, and sail into the late nineteenth century. Newer models, such as the one owned by Morris's son Al, have transoms that are wider and flat. While not as pretty, the new design doesn't suffer from the tendency of the older models to squat low in the stern from the added weight of the engine, a condition remedied by the addition of squat boards, horizontal pieces of wood jutting out from the transom at water level.

"I can tell any boat out here by the rig of her lights," Morris went on, and the feat seemed all the more remarkable because the local boats had no lights. Morris's only concession to Coast Guard Rules of the Road was a dim two-cell flashlight. "I'll just show this up here if I see someone coming," he said.

Once through Kedges Straits, the faint low bluff of Deal Island surfaced from the mists of the Eastern Shore. The breeze freshened as the sky brightened, steepening the swells into rollers. The *Little Doll* nestled into a trough and rode it north, toward Holland Island.

Morris continued: "My grandfather had a skipjack—I crewed on her for five years. There's fourteen skipjacks on Smith Island when I was doing it. Most of them's dead now. Yes, I believe I do prefer scraping peelers to oystering."

Of the seventy-five to a hundred crab scrapers of Smith Island, Morris is probably the local luminary, a celebrity status he wears as easily as his "Little Doll" cap. Among the people he has taken out on his boat are: the Navy Commander Cecil Fox; reporters from Maryland Public TV, "PM Magazine," and Japanese Public TV; and William Warner, author of the Pulitzer Prize-winning *Beautiful Swimmers*.

"I'm chapter nine," said Morris. "Summer and Scraping." Warner retells a day crab scraping with Morris, a day much like any other day in the summertime pattern of Morris's life, a day eleven years before this one. Chapter ten, "The Islands, Looking Ahead," journeys reflectively, speculatively, through the islands of Smith and Tangier, through Crisfield on the Eastern Shore mainland, through the uneasy thoughts of watermen, the foreboding predictions of marine biologists, before it explodes, in its final paragraph, in a comparison that reverberates backward through two hundred and sixty-one pages: "General eutrophication is Lake Erie. Simple as that."

The fear Warner pinned with his comparison was that ever-increasing nutrient loads into the Chesapeake would starve its waters of oxygen—as they had Lake Erie's—and that from the starvation a different, poorer, Bay would emerge, a Bay "leaden and gray," dark, "almost opaque." The fear remains.

On brightening waters crab pot markers dotted the surface. The *Little Doll* rode flattened swells in the lee of Holland Island, where an arc of flat water, shallow and thick with grasses, promised good scraping.

At the dawn of this century, Holland Island sported farm fields and pinewoods, narrow streets and frame houses. Reduced by erosion to one white clapboard house and three or four small cemetery plots, the whole was now owned by a gun club. "This island's washing away fast," Morris said, with evident sadness. "I was crabbing with an old fella here one Saturday. He said his father brought him here when he was a kid. There were five hundred people here for a ball game. Two couldn't stand with their feet dry now. The main cemetery here is two miles out in the water. There's some that comes back for their relatives. Four years ago you could look over this island and not see the Bay." He pointed as he spoke to a section of Holland Island now twenty feet wide. "I hate to see trees wash into the Bay," he went on. "But that's what they're doing."

Morris throttled back the diesel and shifted to neutral. He surveyed the lone clapboard house, the few remaining trees. "I was talking to an old woman who told me about a camp meeting here when that westward bank was fifteen feet high. That was a hundred, a hundred-twenty-five years ago." The westward bank was now inches high and crumbling. "When that bank breaches through, the sand will come and bury the grass. I won't be able to work here then."

He drifted, still watching the fading island. "I was up here one day and saw the biggest eagle I ever saw. I couldn't believe how big it was. Had a good five-foot wing spread, easy, probably six. Head looked like snow. I saw it get off that island and climb. It got so high up I couldn't hardly see it. It circled for five minutes in tight circles, and then headed north."

Morris shed his sweatshirt, then donned his white apron and his black rubber gloves. He fit cross-pieces into the washboards to hold the contents of the scrape. He went forward, untied the scrapes from their braces, and threw them into the water. Ten feet from Holland Island, in two feet of water, Morris began to scrape for crabs.

"When that bank breaches through, the sand will come and bury the grass. I won't be able to work here then."

Now, a little after 7:00, Morris pushed the starboard scrape back in the water, sat on the narrow bench that spanned the back of the open bilge and settled down to cull. Resting on the floorboards, within reach or easy tossing distance, were various buckets and baskets to receive his catch. With great care, he segregated the molting crabs according to their readiness to shed. Peelers he could distinguish by a rim of color around the paddle fin of their seventh appendage, the swimmerette. Green peelers, those five to seven days from shedding, had a red rim. Morris cracked their claws to prevent fighting and tossed them into any of three buckets, one at his feet, the other two scattered about the bilge. Rank peelers, those within three days of peeling, he slipped through a cut piece of carpet into a galvanized bucket beneath the bench. Busters, crabs that had begun shedding (a crack had formed along the margin of the carapace, signaling the beginning of the molt), he placed in a live well mounted on the squat boards.

Far less frequently, Morris found soft crabs tightly wrapped in the grasses, crabs that had already shed but that had not yet hardened. To the eye they were indistinguishable from hard crabs, to the touch they were mud pies. Morris placed them in a bushel basket, where the absence of water would prevent their hardening. The paper shells, crabs that had shed and had already begun to harden, he threw over the side—too hard for the soft-shell market, they were too soft for the hard. Occasionally, as the buckets filled, Morris emptied them into live wells forward of the motor box. He took great care not to bruise them—if overly disturbed they would "hang up" and not shed. He lowered the buckets into the gently churning, aerated well, and slowly spilled out the crabs.

It takes a large man to haul the scrape, and Morris, at six-foot-four and two hundred and seventy-five pounds, seems genetically programmed for the task.

Nearby, as he worked, a larger and deeper boat of unusual rig scraped the same beds. She had a mast and boom equipped with hydraulic winch, and she pulled a single scrape that her captain could haul in with the flick of a lever. New boats had come on in the last few years, and were becoming more popular—they are easier to work, their rig quickly adapted for oystering, allowing watermen to work the same boat year round. Morris didn't think it had much of an advantage. "While he's thinking about it, I can already be turned around," he said. "And I think his propeller does more damage than a scrape can do. Maybe I'll do that when I get old."

From a distance, the captains of the Jenkin's Creekers look unusually large in their small open boats, an impression undisturbed up close. Morris Marsh had had to slit the cuffs of his black rubber gloves to fit them over his massive hands, and his wrap-around apron wouldn't. It takes a large man to haul the scrape, and Morris, at six-foot-four and two hundred and seventy-five pounds, seems genetically programmed for the task, an inheritance passed on to his son Al, who scraped nearby from the *Miss Brenda*. Father and son are built to the same specs—torsos like oak trees and biceps like boulders.

Following on Morris's efforts, also sifting through the grasses, were sea gulls. A loud and loyal entourage of perhaps a dozen attended Morris and the *Little Doll* all day long, picking out grass shrimp and pipe fish and small crabs from the floating grasses thrown overboard moments before. Occasionally a brazen bird would come right onto the washboard. "I'd kill them if I could," Morris said, though his efforts to sweep them away were gentle and slow. One mottled brown immature herring gull stepped sprightly about, waggling its head from side to side, looking for a handout. It craned its neck and peered fearlessly into a pile of muddy green refuse; it picked nonchalantly, its yellow beak a blithely thrusted dagger. Winking and waggling, the gull pranced up to a two-inch crab which raised and spread its opened claws in response. The gull shrieked and flew off.

"That's one thing about those stupid gulls," Morris said. "They know how to fly. They don't fool with it. They'll outmaneuver most birds."

When not hosting journalists and film crews Morris spends his summer days solely in the company of sea gulls. He knows them quite well and their familiarity has bred contempt.

"Sea gulls are genuine stupid," he pointed out, but then went on to argue the contrary case: "They'll come right aboard the boat and take crabs right out of the baskets. Why, they'll even come into the crab house, the herring gulls will. I'd kill them if I could."

~⌒

The crab house, a rough-boarded shanty along the main street of Ewell, across the thoroughfare from where Morris docks his boat, is, like the island itself, accessible only by water. Behind its pier, under its slanting roof, are thirty "crab floats," four- by eight-foot low-walled tanks raised like tables, so called because they derive from the floating lath pens where, until recently, soft crab fishermen put their catch at the end of the day. There the crabs would stay until they had shed. Every six hours around the clock a waterman—or his wife or children—would check the floats to remove newly shed soft crabs. Failure to remove them promptly could result in their being torn apart by crabs not yet shed, or being eaten by sea gulls waiting impatiently overhead. Surviving these threats, the newly shed crab would rapidly harden if not removed, becoming a paper shell with no market.

Smith Island once had hundreds of such floats lining or obstructing every thoroughfare and swale, as did Crisfield, the nearest town on the mainland. But mortality rates were staggering

—up to seventy-five percent of the peelers hung up as they shed, or were eaten by gulls just after. The raised and covered floats Morris now uses are a new design, refined by (among others) Sea Grant Extension agents, the marine equivalent of the more familiar agricultural extension agents. The new floats are safe from predation, except for the occasional stupid herring gull, and the stream of water pumped continuously into them makes for better oxygen mixing and dissipation of wastes, factors contributing to easier shedding. Mortalities are now lower, but may still range up to fifty percent during the warmer months.

The new floats have not appreciably altered the pattern of the crab scraper's work. Now, as before, he pulls his boat up to the crab house at the end of the day and dips out his catch. Now, as before, he packs soft crabs in dried grass and chipped ice, in corrugated trays layered in corrugated boxes, and loads them on the evening ferry to Crisfield, from where they'll be trucked to Baltimore and New York. Now, as before, the peelers are sorted—ranks, greens, busters—and placed in the appropriate tanks for shedding. Now, as before, the floats are tended round the clock, May through October. For Morris, the job is now a little easier than it had been eleven years before. His father-in-law, his son and he banded together to supply a common collection of floats serviced by a fourth man whose job was to to tend them, and who worked on shares along with the rest of them.

This way of fishing, the scraping for soft-shell crabs, the tending of floats, the sending to market, is of obscure origin and is practiced nowhere else on such a scale.

This way of fishing, the scraping for soft-shell crabs, the tending of floats, the sending to market, is of obscure origin and is practiced nowhere else on such a scale. When the Bureau of Fisheries of the United States, an early forerunner of the National Marine Fisheries Service, undertook its immense survey of America's fisheries in 1879, a survey of a scale and scope not ventured since, it poked into every nook and cranny of every waterside town that engaged in any fishing at all. Of soft crabbing, it noted that most softs were taken incidentally by hard crab fishermen who put them in shore pens, fenced-off areas in shallow water. But the shore pens must have been difficult to work, for around 1855, in New Jersey, "shedding cars" were introduced. They were of a design similar to what would later be used in Maryland, where they would be called floats. The only fishing then specific to softs was dip netting—with the blunt end of a dip net, watermen dipped out crabs they could see on the bottom. It's a method still practiced on Smith Island, and elsewhere around the Bay, though mainly by retirees and recreational crabbers.

By noon Morris had been scraping for six hours and would be scraping for another three before heading back to the shanty. He pulled on the port scrape. It pulled back. He pulled again, wincing. When at last he had the frame alongside and heaved onto the washboard, he said, "There's too much grass now. It floats around so you can hardly work." The great seagrass decline of the Chesapeake had gone unnoticed in Tangier Sound. "It's laying on top of the water in most places. You can't crab. It's been more scattered than it used to be way back, but it's too thick. You work here and you can't imagine a shortage of grass. If you could spread it out, the Bay'd be covered with it."

In the port scrape were two greens, one rank, and two softs. With three scapers contributing to the shanty, the operation's total catch for the day would approach forty dozen.

Out of high school and working alongside his father, Al, now seventeen years old, was six when Morris took William Warner crab scraping. There was talk then that Al might leave the cycle of working the water, might go to college, to a future not tied to the water. The options were still open, but for now, with his new Jenkin's Creeker, his new GMC diesel, his mildly Elizabethan accent, Al is nothing if not perfectly fitted for crab scraping. Like his father, he scrapes for peelers, rank and green, busters, and a way of life bound to the seagrasses.

ANOTHER DAY ON THE BAY

Upper Bay, Early September, 9:00 A.M.

Aboard the *Bad Boy's Toy*, thirty-seven feet of fiberglassed, stripped-planked Cedar Robins Chesapeake Bay deadrise. On a rough, uncertain day—winds east-northeast at twenty knots; a frontal system poised to sweep down from the north with higher winds, lightning and showers, eighty-five degrees, and wet rag humid—the workboat bounded through the waves, four-foot rollers, and slapped into the troughs.

"It's going to blow thirty before it stops," Danny Beck shouted as he throttled back the Jimmy and gaffed a pot. A red light flashed, an alarm bell sounded, the *Bad Boy's Toy* bucked and shuttered and slowed. The light and alarm, which indicated that the engine—a GMC diesel, otherwise known as a Jimmy—was going too slow for efficient oil circulation, had been flashing and screaming intermittently since 5:00 A.M. and, together with the roll of the deck, the splash of the waves and the wind, made for an all-out assault on the senses. Crab potting Danny Beck-style was enough to make one green and vertiginous, ejective. But Danny Beck, standing erect at the starboard rail, gaff in one hand, engine lever in the other, was unafflicted.

Anyone who hangs around the Chesapeake where watermen gather is sure to hear of Danny Beck. He works harder than most anybody—does more kinds of fishing, works longer hours, drives harder. And he's not shy with his opinions—opinions targeted mainly on the Maryland Department of Natural Resources, which, Danny Beck feels, has defrauded him out of his yearly allotment of rockfish, and which, he'll point out without much provocation, is made up of "pimps and whores" and "communist bastards."

Danny's antipathy to those who would regulate his work, his "whole way of life," comes naturally to him and needs no rationale. Nonetheless, he has one.

The story, from Danny Beck's perspective, is this: In 1984, amid steadily declining striper harvests and pressures from other states in the loose compact called the Atlantic States Fisheries Commission to reduce or eliminate the harvest, the Department of Natural Resources mandated a fifty-five percent reduction in catch for Maryland's portion of the Chesapeake Bay, the largest rockfish nursery on the East Coast. In a rare instance of cooperation the watermen willingly complied and reduced their catches. And the department, pleased with the result, told the watermen that there'd be no further regulation needed and they should go ahead and purchase nets for the 1985 season. But then, as Danny remembers it, on the eleventh of September a letter came in the mail over the signature of Dr. Torrey Brown, department secretary, to the effect that a total striper moratorium would be imposed the following January, and would last an indefinite period determined only by the number of stripers spawned in the Bay.

Danny's response to this about-face illuminates the best known aspect of his character. On the fourteenth of September, at a meeting convened by Dr. Brown to explain his department's intentions, Danny got up and made his feelings clear. Influencing those feelings was a lump on his back of unexamined malevolence. Midway through the meeting Danny stood up, turned around, lifted his shirt, and exposed his lump. Looking backward over his shoulder, addressing the podium, where Dr. Brown and his assistant, Dr. George Krantz, stood listening, he said, "You see that lump on my back? I'm going to get that thing examined after this moratorium law goes into effect, and if the son of a bitch is cancer, before I die and go to hell, I'm going to take you two bastards with me." Danny Beck thereupon walked out. In attendance at the next meeting were swarms of Marine Police officers, their holsters unlatched.

"It's just a common day," Danny wailed as he throttled up the diesel in reverse. "Just another day on the Chesapeake." A buoy swirled past in an eddy of wave wash. Danny thrusted his gaff—fluidly, nonchantly—hooked the buoy's warp and passed it down the washboard to Chuck, who wrapped the warp around the hydraulic puller, grabbed the pot when it broke the surface, inverted its contents into a low trough, stuffed a mud shad in the pot's bait box, and tossed the pot back over the side. Chuck spoke little as he worked and when he did his voice came out garbled—his face was swollen, his lip badly cut, slightly mangled, a little askew, the result of a bar fight on Baltimore's famed Block.

What spilled into the trough were crabs—seven Jimmies, three Number Twos, six Whites and four sooks. Aboard the *Bad Boy's Toy* Whites were the rough equivalent of Number Threes and were so called because the underside of their newly hardened shells shimmered like titanium, too new to be fouled by the water. Whites fetch a low price—they don't have much meat for their size.

One at each side of the trough, long tongs at the ready, Fred and Daren picked out the scampering crabs and tossed them into the appropriate baskets, adding to a catch that already exceeded fourteen bushels. Fred, Chuck's father, is a retired plumbing fixture salesman from Baltimore, who, like his son, had been crewing the *Bad Boy's Toy* for years. Daren, the youngest and newest to this line of work, was giving commercial fishing a try.

The pace was hyperkinetic; there were *six hundred* pots to run, to gaff, to empty, to rebait and reset on the bottom. There was no time to lose; there was time only to run the next pot, and the one after.

"It's going to blow our ass off today," Danny shouted into the freshening breeze as he gaffed the next pot. The white spray from a wave crest shot up the hull and splashed his face. Droplets of water dribbled from his beard onto his bulging bib.

"Oooo-weee! I don't make a lot of money but I have a lot of fun." Trapped in the next-to-last pot, its flanks shimmering, its alabaster belly opalescing, was a twenty-four-inch striped bass—striper, Maryland State Fish. "You see, here's one of those endangered species," Danny

"Oooo-weee! I don't make a lot of money but I have a lot of fun."

wailed. "I usually cut them up for bait." Daren threw it over the side. In the last pot of the row were two Number Ones, three Number Twos and two sooks. As Chuck tossed the pot over the side Danny throttled up the *Bad Boy's Toy*, and turned north toward the next row of pots.

～

Crabbing by pot is new to the Chesapeake, barely fifty years old, adolescent compared to many other Bay fisheries. The first Chesapeake-style crab pot is said to have been invented in Virginia in the 1930s, though the idea itself is much older (traps for catching various marine animals date back to earliest recorded history). The first pots were baskets of tightly woven wicker, often in the shape of vases. Their use was recorded by Herodotus, the father of history, who, writing in the fifth century B.C., told of the staked hut dwellers of Lake Prasias, where fish were so bountiful that "a man has only to open his trap door, and let down a basket by a rope into the water, and then wait a very short time, when he draws it up quite full of fish." Plato, in a prayer for a young man (from *The Laws*), urged that "no desire of hunting in the sea, or of catching the creatures in the waters, ever take possession of you, either when you are awake, or when you are asleep, by hooks, with weels, which latter is a very lazy contrivance. . . ." (Lest there be any doubt in the minds of young male Greeks about his instructions, Plato went on to say that fishing "is not an occupation worthy of a man well born or well brought up, because it demands more of address and ruse than force, and is not for young people. . . .") The lazy and morally corrosive contrivance "weels" was an English translation, the word a development from willy, itself taken from willow, of which many English eel pots have for centuries been made. Pots of varying design and construction were probably used whenever the fishermen who tried them found they worked—wicker for eels, ceramic for octopus, lath for fish and crabs and lobsters, wire for blue crabs.

The Chesapeake crab pot, a wire mesh cube thirty inches on a side, is made of wire mesh because blue crabs will not enter darkened pots. The crab enters through one of four side funnels into a bottom section, attracted by menhaden or mud shad tantalizingly encased in a wire mesh box. Once inside, feeling the ominous sense of its own confinement, the crab swims upward, as troubled crabs are wont to do, through an opening between two upward-sweeping wire mesh flaps, into an upper section, from which it has no escape except the way it came, which is down, a direction troubled crabs don't travel.

The pots are expensive. A specially galvanized wire netting is used in their construction, and the construction is by hand. Metal rebar wraps the perimeter of the bottom, to keep the bottom side down, and a sacrificial anode of pure zinc is fastened to forestall corrosion. All this together contributes to a twenty-dollar-per-pot price tag, complete with warp and buoy. An average potter scatters several hundred pots on the Chesapeake's floor, an investment of several thousand dollars.

"I started with eighteen hundred and fifty, but never set six hundred, seeing as it was going to be a long year right off the bat," Danny said from his perch on the captain's chair while en route to the next row. Of the remaining twelve hundred and fifty, he ran a set of about six hundred each day, alternating sets day by day. The standard galvanized netting used on pots elsewhere in the Chesapeake with considerable success was not suitable to Danny and he built his own out of heavier material. One-by-ones and two-by-twos, he called his pots, after the dimensions of the heavy wire hardware cloth he used to build them. He used heavier pots because he fished in and around the Aberdeen Proving Grounds, where naval ordnance is routinely tested (not far from where Chuckie Clark often fished eel pots).

"Chicken wire pots don't last up here," Danny said. "The zincs don't work as well in these fresher waters. Aberdeen has one million tons of iron in the water—been shooting there since 1923—and it's all lying there. That creates a hell of a lot of electrolysis up there. Ain't nothing but a waste, a damn dump."

The time between rows was also time for lunch, fried bluefish Danny had caught the previous evening while haul seining for carp. Danny seines carp for the "Jewish Holiday market." The carp are ground and used, together with whitefish, in the making of gefilte fish. "I seen them clean them sons a bitches and they use everything but the eyes and one fin. But that market ain't what it used to be. Younger Jewish people don't mess with it." He also intended soon to pound net for catfish and perch, if he could find his way into the relatively closed market. That would give more balance to his year, which now consisted of crabbing in the summer and spending his winters making pots and "picking shit with the chickens." Danny needed to balance his year on the water because he couldn't fish for stripers.

"You got to try and think like a crab all the time. All the things that can affect them, you got to think about almost every day."

Whenever that thought occurred to him his mental outrage was immediately directed at the Department of Natural Resources, and its regulation of watermen, regulation he likened to America's earlier treatment of Indians.

"They'd like to drive us right off this Bay is what they'd like. Just like the Indians. They took seventy-five to eighty thousand dollars' worth of income and two hundred thousand dollars' worth of gear away from me. And for compensation they gave out ten thousand—it's a bone to a dog."

The compensation came from a state program offered, together with the news of the moratorium, to Maryland's striper fishermen by the Department of Natural Resources. For taking aboard a department scientist and surveying the oyster bars of the upper Bay, Danny is paid by the day, by the State of Maryland. Danny once took out one of the department's higher level administrators, who, to judge from Danny's recollection of the encounter, probably never made another trip: "I took one look at that son of a bitch and asked him whether he's to be rowed or throwed."

~⌒

Off Pooles Island, 11:00 A.M. The winds were rising and the waves were quick to follow. The crabs were slow to the pots, as they had been all year in the upper Bay. "We should be getting a bushel of everything every ten pots," Danny shouted as he gaffed another pot. "And if you get a bushel every fifteen to twenty, then they better be Number Ones."

From the last row of one hundred and sixty-one pots Danny got six-and-a-half bushels, for an average of one bushel every twenty-five pots. Crab potting was not going well, and with all that investment lying around slowly corroding on the Bay floor, the temptation to take extreme and regressive measures to find crabs can be irresistible. "You got to try and think like a crab all the time," Danny said. "Try to outfigure them. All the things that can affect them, you got to think about almost every day. I move some of my pots further down the Bay, then it picked up up here. I never put pots below the Bay bridge, but it wouldn't matter if I did—it's been poor all over, everywhere. Don't nobody know where the crabs are."

Where the crabs were nobody knew, but where they had been apparently extended way below the Bay bridge and out into the Atlantic, a factor that may account for their recurring numbers amid the declines of other species. In the 1970s pioneering work by scientists at the University of Maryland's Horn Point Environmental Laboratory, the University of Delaware's College of Marine Studies and Virginia's Old Dominion University focused on where the crabs likely were when they weren't in the pots. It was known that in the winter the males burrowed down into the mud of the nearest deep channel and that many of the females scurried down to burrow near the mouth of the Bay. It was also known that crabs, including those quite juvenile, began moving up the Bay in the spring.

The questions centered on the several-month gap in the crabs' life cycle—on where the crabs were between late autumn and spring, where they were born, and where they had traveled afterward.

Steve Sulkin, a University of Maryland scientist, sought to answer these questions, to assign places and times to the crabs' travelogue, by studying the response of laboratory-reared crab larvae to stimuli modeled on conditions crabs would naturally find in the Bay. Assisted by co-workers and graduate students, Sulkin took blue crab larvae from three age classes—those just hatched, those just shy of their final larval molt and a group midway between—and exposed them first to light. He found that the youngest larvae swam toward the light, and that the oldest swam away. He then exposed the larvae to changes in temperature, to changes in salinity, to changes in the apparent position of the earth relative to the larvae. What he learned from all these experiments was that the youngest larvae preferred, and actively sought, conditions such as they would find naturally occurring in the upper layers of the Bay's stratified waters, the outgoing, Atlantic-bound waters, and that the the older larvae sought conditions similar to those they would find in the bottom, bayward-flowing waters of the Chesapeake.

Meanwhile, Charles Epifanio, of the University of Delaware's College of Marine Studies, and Anthony J. Provenzano, of Virginia's Old Dominion University, were verifying that blue crab larvae actually do flow outward to the Atlantic when young, and back toward the Delaware and Chesapeake bays when older.

What emerged from all this painstaking research was the discovery that the shelf waters of the mid-Atlantic coast are a kind of mixing bowl for crab larvae that had come from rivers and bays all along the coast, and that whether and how many larvae would return to a particular bay—to the Albemarle, the Pamlico, the Chesapeake, the Delaware—would depend on winds and waves and currents. The management implications of these discoveries were unsettling —Maryland blue crabs are Virginia blue crabs are Delaware blue crabs; of a suprastate community, they travel with diplomatic immunity and can't be regulated in their home waters.

Also revealed by these discoveries was a likely reason for the blue crabs continuing abundance during a period of continually eroding water quality and declines in other estuarine species. Blue crabs, unlike stripers, herring or shad, spend their most delicate, developing moments out in the Atlantic, where recreational boaters may flush their toilets but where dilution in oceanic volumes ensures that the waters remain relatively clean.

Coming into Hawk Cove, 2:00 P.M. Aboard the *Bad Boy's Toy* were forty-four bushels of crabs —fifteen Number Ones, nine Number Twos, four Whites, and sixteen sooks. Captain and crew had variously settled into their preferred modes of repose—Fred stretched out napping on the motor box, Chuck and Daren dozing on benches in the cabin, Danny slumped over the wheel, apparently asleep. The *Bad Boy's Toy* passed through the narrow channel leading past Hart Island into Hawk Cove without incident.

When Danny brings home his catch, a new workday looms before him. Unlike most watermen, Danny doesn't bring his catch back to a buyer waiting in a shiny new truck. "Crabber-buyer relationship is much the same as a pimp and his girls," he said. "We do all the work, he gets all the money." So when Danny gets back to his dock, he loads up *his* truck and sets out to market his crabs himself. He sells to several restaurants directly, and to a couple of commercial fish outlets. He does the same job that the buyer would do and thus captures for himself a layer of profit usually taken by them. "When you got a crab house, you got a license to steal one-third right automatically," he says.

Danny's pier juts into Brown's creek, near Essex, just north of Baltimore. At waterside it resembles any Eastern Shore dock, an impression immediately dispelled by southerly winds—they carry the sulfuric effusions of Baltimore's Sparrows Point steel plant. Visible on Danny's dock now, in daylight, were thirteen feed sacks (forty-five kilograms each of coarse cracked corn), seven poly barrels, bushel baskets, crab pots, culling board, fuel pump, several five-gallon cans, a box of empty oil jugs (Drydene), water pump and hose, prop, net, anchor and battery. Tied to and near the dock were two other boats, and a third was out in the creek. All this gear kept Danny on the water, potting for crabs, fishing for carp, perhaps soon for catfish, eventually, he hoped, for stripers.

As he pulled up to the dock, at 2:30, having put in his eight hours as a fisherman, Danny readied for another work day as a trucker. "Breezing up northwest here now," he said. "Shit, I guess it's going to blow our ass off again tomorrow. It's been a lousy season. It may pick up more in October. It may get better when the crabs come out of the rivers. I don't know yet. But, hey, I'm high on life—I don't care what the crabs do."

IGNORANT STICKS

Nanticoke River, October, 9:00 A.M.

A board the *Elvira Ann*—Ben Waters, his back ramrod straight yet angled slightly forward, his center of mass further outboard than prudence would recommend, raised his tongs hand over hand along the wooden shafts. He muscled the heads up to the water's surface, reached low for the rivet pin and heaved the heads clear of the water, the shafts, pivoting on the fulcrum of his right hand, scribing a counterclockwise arc in their sweep. He worked at the very edge of the *Elvira Ann*, balanced on the washboard, a narrow strip of deck that ran the length of the cockpit along both sides. It was narrower than his feet were long—two inches of boot and toe cantilevered over the Nanticoke River. He turned forward, cocked his knees inboard, and swung the tong heads over the culling board, where he opened them slightly to release his catch. "This is the year of the shell," he said as he swung the heads back over the water and eased his grip on the shafts.

It was not, for Ben Waters and his brothers Grant and Earl, the year of the oyster.

With a muffled splash, the heads dropped through the surface; the wet shafts glided silently through black rubber gloves; a slight rustle could be heard as the heads bottomed on the oyster rock fifteen feet below. Ben spread the shafts and scissored them back and forth nine or ten times, raking together a small mound of shells and oysters; the sound was that of a rake drawn

OYSTERS:
HAND
TONGING

through chipped stone. He closed the shafts and lifted them, hand over hand, his shoulders rising and falling like slow-motion pistons.

Ben's tongs were made of yellow-pine, two shafts bolted at their lower ends to opposing steel rod half-cylindrical baskets, called heads, and pinned together with a rivet, in the manner of a pair of scissors. Called hand tongs, or shaft tongs, they are—as they have been for two-and-a-half centuries—the principal device for harvesting the Chesapeake's oysters.

Ben learned to tong oysters about fifty-five years ago when he was about eighteen. "I had done farming, working as a hand during the harvests. But my daddy was a waterman, you know, and it was more or less like father like son. And that was practically the only thing around this area that you become interested in."

"This area" is Nanticoke, a community of four hundred, clustered around a rectangular, bulk-headed harbor on the lower reaches of the Nanticoke River on Maryland's lower Eastern Shore. Split in equal measures between farmers and fishermen, blacks and whites, Nanticoke spreads out along both shoulders of a two-lane that cuts through truck farms and grain fields on its way from Salisbury to Bivalve and Nanticoke and Waterview. The end of the road is Stump Point, a desolate, loblollied tongue of land jutting into Tangier Sound. Scattered frame houses set amid corn and soybean fields, old-growth loblolly pines and oaks and the occasional derelict chicken coop, give way slowly to marsh, a small bridge, then the town limits of Nanticoke. Missing is a proper grocery (the nearest substitute being the West-End Mini-Mart just outside town) and a gas station (Texaco having moved out some time ago). No other signs of commerce line the harbor except for Kennerly Booth and Sea-Pak, two seafood shippers. The only brick building is the United States Post Office (zip code 21840). By Eastern Shore tradition, there are two Methodist churches, each an Asbury United Methodist Church, one for white parishoners, the other for black. Ben and his family worship every Sunday, and often during the week, at the latter. Except for two winters spent working for a "private family" in Philadelphia, Ben has lived and worked all of his seventy-three years in Nanticoke, leaving at dawn most winter mornings, over the last five-and-a-half decades, to tong for oysters.

The day had started at 7:00. The Nanticoke harbor lights were yellow vignettes in heavy mist hung suspended above a harbor that was not only, at seventy degrees, unseasonably warm, but also humid and foggy. Ben pulled his Chevy pickup into an assigned space facing the harbor, nose to nose with the *Elvira Ann*. He climbed down from the cab, ambled around to the open tailgate, and dragged out three bushels of shucked oyster shells. Grant and Earl drove up in a low-slung Chevy sedan. Earl, who works the night cleaning crew for Kennerly Booth, sometimes until 4:00 in the morning, does not find this a time for animated conversation. Bag lunches in hand, Grant and Earl came onto the finger pier, stepped down to the washboard and

jumped into the cockpit, without speaking a word. Ben heaved the bushels of shells down to Grant, who stacked them forward, next to the cabin. Earl cranked the aging eight-cylinder Buick engine, slipped the aft line from the piling and, throwing the transmission lever into reverse, eased the *Elvira Ann* back from her slip into the still harbor. Then he motored past the jetty and onto the Nanticoke, a broad somnolent flood-plain river letting into Tangier Sound.

The shells Ben brought along were from oysters he had tonged and shucked for a revival meeting. "Lot of people go to camp meetings," he said from the small cockpit of the *Elvira Ann*. "They go to get oyster fritters and then go back to their cars, and go on about their business." Leaving go the souls, the shells he saves, returning them to the Nanticoke, where they would serve as cultch—the hard substrate that next summer's larval oysters would settle on when they metamorphosed into pinhead-sized oysters called spat.

Earl throttled back the Buick and shifted to neutral. The *Elvira Ann* drifted southwest of the harbor, above five acres of oyster bar that Ben leased from the State of Maryland. Leased beds are prevalent in the Nanticoke as they are nowhere else in Maryland, where they've never reached the level of importance they enjoy in Virginia. For all that, they're quite important to Nanticoke watermen, offering, as they do, the major source of summer employment—unlike the public bars, leased beds can be worked year round.

Ben and Grant hauled the baskets up to the combing and spilled the shells over the side. Turning westward, Earl headed the *Elvira Ann* toward midstream, and cruised for a few minutes. He throttled back the Buick and reached for a broken tong shaft to check the depth and the texture of the bottom. Feeling hard bottom at fourteen feet, he cut the motor. Grant threw overboard a thirty-pound scrap of iron casting as anchor, donned a dark green rubberized bib and black rubber gloves and stationed himself forward of the culling board, a wide, two-sided trough that runs athwartships just forward of the motorbox, facing aft. Earl and Ben put on gloves, selected the right length pair of tongs from the pile of six, and ascended the washboards, Ben the starboard, Earl the port, steadying themselves with the tongs like tightrope walkers. The work began.

Earlier oyster gatherers, Nanticoke Indians, waded out to oyster bars at low tide, their feet swaddled in hides, and plucked the oysters, which they opened by roasting over coals or with knives chipped from stone. The more adventurous Indians dove from the surface, returning oysters by the handful to canoes burned and scraped from the loblolly pines that rimmed the river. This was also the pattern for the arriving Europeans, but it didn't last. On the flood tide of European immigration came increasing harvests that soon depleted the shallow water oyster beds near shore. The settlers then turned toward deeper water. These events are recorded in oyster shell piles left in privies and trash pits of the early settlers. Oysters that grow in shallow waters, called cove oysters, have delicate, feathery undulations along the margins of their thin shells. Those from deeper waters are smoother, more elongate and robust. Around 1720 these more robust shells began appearing in shell piles—the settlers had learned to tong them.

"They've caught most of them off the hard bottom. You got to pick around now to where you think the oysters are."

And now, at 9:00, Ben and Earl dropped their tongs through the Nanticoke's surface and heaved them back from its floor. What they spilled onto the culling board was nothing anyone would think to eat. It was mostly shells, old half oyster shells covered with watery green-brown mud and the occasional sea squirt, a translucent, sac-like animal that squirts a stream of water when touched. In among and on the shells were also small ribbed mussels, half-inch oyster spat from last spring's strike, some flatworms, and a couple skilletfish, a small forager of isopods. Conspicuously absent were three-inch keepable oysters. Ben paused momentarily, his eyes focused on the culling board as Grant sorted through the refuse. "This is a bad way to make a living," he said.

Earl laid his tongs beside the motorbox, started the Buick and moved a short way upstream, dragging anchor. "We're just looking for a few more on the bottom," said Ben, as Earl backed the throttle and again checked the river floor with the broken shaft. This would be the pattern for the morning—motor from one spot to another, looking for a few more on the bottom, usually not finding many. "They've caught most of them off the hard bottom. You got to pick around

now to where you think the oysters are," Ben went on. The season for shaft tonging opened September fifteenth, a month ago, and the public oyster bars were already picked over.

Satisfied with the feel of the bottom, Earl turned off the motor. The *Elvira Ann* rebounded gently on her anchor rode, swaying ten feet above the oyster bar. Ben shed his sweatshirt, climbed the washboard and spread the shafts. The first lick up was Earl's and its contents looked slightly more promising. In among the shells were clumps of oysters and shells cemented together and covered with blisters. Unlikely omens, these muddy green conglomerates, but their presence was a welcome sign; it meant this bed was not as worked as the prior one, where loose shells bore witness to a prior encounter with someone else's culling hammer.

Grant's hammer was of welded steel; along its barrel were two prongs that measured out three inches, legal minimum size set by Maryland state law. Grant wielded the hammer as a carpenter would, using it to knock apart the clumps, breaking the shells and undersized oysters off the keepable oysters, which he tossed forward of the culling board, forming a mound in front of the motorbox. After hauling up fifteen licks apiece, Ben and Earl had amassed barely one bushel of oysters, a small pyramid on the cockpit sole ten inches high.

For all the effort the oysters mounded up slowly. Ben and Earl paused frequently and looked down at the culling board, wistfully. They knew without looking how the catch was going. They felt it in the weight of the tongs—live, flesh- and fluid-filled oyters are much heavier than shells. They heard it in the sound made as oysters fell onto the culling board—half shells and boxes (closed shells filled with mud) made a light clattering sound; whole, live oysters dropped with an authoritative thump. Grant's job was easy—there were few oyster clumps to separate or marginal oysters to measure. For each haul dumped onto the culling board, he broke apart a single clump, tossed two, maybe three oysters onto the mound, then placed his hands on edge, fingertip to palm, and swept the rest of the muddy pile overboard.

Oysters are always culled aboard the boat and above the bed. State law requires it, and prudence necessitates it. Cemented to the culled shells are smaller oysters that will provide harvests for next year and the years to follow. The shells also provide cultch, where next season's newly setting oysters will attach.

Lick by lick, a fair portion of Wilson Shoals, the oyster bar the brothers worked, had crossed the culling board by 9:30, and they had barely two bushels of keepable oysters to show for it. The atmosphere on board was listless and reflective, lacking momentum or energy. Ben interspersed his licks with somber reflection:

"You never know what you're going to make. This is just a haphazard job. We had a fella here who used to call them ignorant sticks.

"Most kids now trying to get a job more permanent than this.

"Were I a younger man I'd do something different.

"We just wait it out. There's nothing else to do.

"Trust your luck and hope the Lord will ease up . . .

"Earl, what's we gonna do, son?"

"Let's you and I go bootlegging. We'd make more money than we will at this."

Another move, this time with greater conviction: Grant hauled anchor; Earl turned upstream and opened up the throttle, the *Elvira Ann* shuddering and creaking in response.

Typical of a smaller and older class of Chesapeake workboat, the *Elvira Ann* is thirty-two feet long and six wide. Her keel settles on the mud when the tide leaves less than eighteen inches of water. With her flaking, faded white and green paint and rusting fittings, she appears to have been scuttled, partially restored, and in danger of another immersion—the automatic bilge pump shoots out a steady stream of water for ten minutes out of every hour. Her cockpit is long and low-sided, a workspace two-thirds the length of the boat. Forward is a small cabin with two berths that conform to the angle of the boat's planking, meeting at their forward ends, V berths.

If the Waters brothers had to travel far for oysters, as they did the season of '66 to '67, when local oyster bars were decimated by disease, they would sleep aboard on these berths for a week at a time, returning home on weekends for a soft bed. Now, with oysters again living in the Nanticoke, the berths were loaded with the usual workboat inventory. The cabin was a collage of rust reds and sediment grays, as cluttered as a suburban garage—an Aladdin kerosene heater, life preservers, two old, no-longer-serviceable batteries, coiled ropes of oakum caulking, holed rubber gloves, a ring buoy, two fire extinguishers, and miscellaneous tools caked in rust covered the bare plywood and cedar planks.

10:00 A.M. Billowy cumulus clouds scudded before a breeze that had backed around to the southeast. The opaque gray water picked up a light chop, giving the *Elvira Ann* a slight roll, making the footing on the washboards difficult. Earl throttled back the Buick, checked the bottom nine or ten times, then cocked an eyebrow at Grant, who dropped anchor. One hundred yards to the west was Ragged Point, a low, marshy extrusion from the Nanticoke's otherwise solid east bank, below—seven feet of water.

The first couple of licks were good-sized but mostly of shell.   Ben looked skyward and repeated: "This is a bad way to make a living," drawing the attention of a tonger in a small outboard boat about twenty-five yards to the east, who nodded in agreement.   Ben yelled out to him:

"Let's you and I go bootlegging. We'd make more money than we will at this." A running dialogue ensued that covered hunting ducks and deer, trotlining crabs, the vagaries of the oyster market. They were talking it up like former classmates at the ten-year reunion, like cousins or long-lost friends.

 After about twenty minutes, Ben said: "Hey Cap, you a Bradley?"

"No, I'm a Paul, William Paul."

William Paul worked alone from a boat that was shorter than his tongs were long. He tonged until his culling board was mounded high with oysters, until it seemed the very next gust would surely overturn his wide, top-heavy little boat. Then he stopped to cull. In this manner he would gather four or five bushels to sell to "private clients." He had been doing this since he was twelve. He was now seventy-six.

It is so unlikely, this manner of making a living, this way of harvesting oysters. Huge masses of shells and mud brought up lick by lick, each yielding maybe one oyster, maybe three, a handful. As in panning for gold, mountainous volumes are drawn, examined, and returned, less a precious few valuable lumps. The inefficiency is legislated, the elected officials of Maryland and Virginia having long since realized that more efficient gears, such as were used to excess in more northerly waters during the last century, would eliminate the oyster here as surely as they did in New York and Connecticut. In all of Wicomico County, one of twelve Maryland counties bordering the Chesapeake Bay, the only legal way to take oysters from public beds is by shaft tong. This is also true for tributary rivers throughout the Bay.

Despite the inefficiency, more oysters by far are taken from the Bay by shaft tong than by any other method. Two-thirds of the one and a half million bushels of Maryland oysters taken during the 1985-1986 season were hauled up by hand tong. Slightly over three thousand oystermen worked over one hundred thousand man-days, over thirty days to a man, to harvest those million bushels. The value of the catch was about ten million dollars, leaving each shaft tonger, on average, a seasonal salary of just over three thousand dollars. A haphazard way to make a living.

By 11:00 it was again time to move. Earl motored fifty yards northward, squarely in the middle of Wilson Shoals. Ben dropped the broken shaft to the oyster rock below only once, then reached for his tongs.

The first licks brought to the surface were visibly heavier, the noise they made on the culling board more solid. Ben tossed a black plastic antifreeze bottle as buoy to mark the spot for later reference. They pulled up large licks quickly. Although the heaving was harder, Ben and Earl worked faster, suggesting, in the intensity of their efforts, a determination to catch what oysters were there while they could, as if the oysters could get up and walk away.

Culling took on a furious pace. Grant now moved in biomechanical syncopation, a Charlie Chaplin on an assembly line: right arm, attached to hammer, pounding; left arm, attached to oyster, throwing. Not only was it faster paced, Grant's work now required more discrimination—there were many oysters to measure, many clumps to separate. The oysters mounded up on the culling board faster than Grant could cull them.

Ben and Earl now worked with smooth regularity, a steady rhythm of tongs rising and falling in unison, the shafts scribing out opposing arcs at the same frequency, like large windshield wipers. The mood on board brightened. As they worked they traded comments:

"First time we got oysters like this in a little while."

"Last year was a good year. So was the one before that. Who knows?"

"You got to take luck for them. You can't see them."

"That's one thing about oysters—they don't have feet. They don't walk."

"I brought up many a lick."

"These are nice-looking oysters—makes you feel good all over."

"Oysters. I love them anyway."

A lone loon, one hundred yards to the north, floated, then preened, then dived to the oyster rock below. Thirty, then fifty, then sixty-seven seconds down, it surfaced and floated and preened and dove again. Its time on the surface between dives approached twenty seconds, its dives always upward of a minute, with choreographed regularity. Ben said they dive for toadfish, an ugly, barbeled, loose-jowled and fat-headed fish that preys upon young oysters, crushing them in its massive jaws. The loon may have been preying on oysters too, wrenching the delicate shells from their beds and crushing them, extracting the meat, spitting out shards.

The loon lingered on for about an hour, leaving just as Ben pulled up the last lick and set his tongs beside the motorbox. The brothers took brooms, dunked them into the Nanticoke and swept the washboards, culling board and cockpit sole. Buckets of water were then splashed about to complete the cleanup.

Grant hauled anchor; Earl headed south, toward Nanticoke. As the *Elvira Ann* rounded the jetty, Earl slowed the Buick for the next-to-last time that day, and threw the transmission lever back toward center. The *Elvira Ann* drifted alongside the siding of Kennerly Booth. Slipping broad flat-edged shovels into the mound on the cockpit sole, Ben and Earl loaded oysters by the shovelful into a legally prescribed standard-measure steel bucket that hung from a boom at the dock. The measures were counted off and dumped into five-foot cubic steel wire crates. Money was exchanged, the day was over.

The Waters brothers took up about five hundred licks all told, and brought in seventeen bushels of oysters, which, at nine dollars a bushel, brought them forty-five dollars apiece for the day's efforts, for this, an average day working the water. There would be a market the following

"So many things against you. Rain, snow, sleet—it's all against you."

day. The year would end on these terms—the catches would be small and would bring little money. Hopes would run high for a continued market through the end of the season and for better catches the following spring.

During the 1986-1987 season, for the first time ever, Maryland's oyster harvest dropped below one million bushels.

It's everywhere reported how independent a lot are watermen. But, truth is, watermen trade one set of dependencies for a much harsher group of others. Chief among them is the weather. As friend or foe, the weather's presence is strongly felt. Over the long haul, the weather regulates the oyster harvest. Oyster larvae need saline waters to settle; that means dry springs favor a larger oyster crop two or three years later. Over the short term, the weather easily comes to seem downright conspiratorial: "So many things against you. Rain, snow, sleet—it's all against you." If there's ice on the washboards, you can't work. If the wind blows over twenty knots, you can't work. If the river is hiding beneath ten inches of ice, you can't work. It's not that you'd rather stay home, it's not that you're not quite up to a day out of doors. You can't work—you'll slip off the washboard, you'll be blown or thrown into the water, the boat can't clear the harbor. Your income for the day is zero.

For the coming year, trouble would come mainly from the weather, a rainless stretch that would soon be known as a hundred-year drought. The dry weather would be welcome early in the summer, when the oysters were spawning—such dry weather increases the salinity of the water, an increase that was propitious for larval oysters. But as the summer wore on the drought continued and the salinities increased further, increased until they reached twenty-two parts per thousand in the Nanticoke River, a full five above normal. Dermo and MSX, two parasitic diseases that ravage oyster beds in higher salinities, would sweep through the leased and public bars of the Nanticoke River and kill off most of the juvenile oysters and many of the adults as well. The three bushels of oyster shell that Ben had laid down day would attract plenty of spat, as would the thousand bushels he bought from Kennerly Booth and laid down the following spring, but disease would leave his bed rich in cultch but poor in oysters. During the 1986-1987 season, for the first time ever, Maryland's oyster harvest dropped below one million bushels.

The summer, a time when Ben would normally be out tonging on the Nanticoke's leased beds, left him scrambling for work. He tried painting in Salisbury and around Nanticoke, but there really wasn't much work to be found, and by July he had time on his hands and uncertain prospects for the future.

The drive into Nanticoke that July was through fields of parched and stunted corn. Ben Waters hadn't found much paying work and was painting the Methodist church. The atmosphere was oppressive in its heat and dryness and seemed to weigh heavily on Ben's spirits. He walked down the church steps with a heavy, lumbering gait, dressed not for church but for labor. "I'm hurting, to tell you the truth. I am really. There isn't too much work available in the summertime. The scarcity of oysters on private beds means no work there. Next year I'll probably try crabbing. My boat isn't working now. And it's going to cost some money to fix it up—it takes all the money you can get to live now. It takes me all the money I can get to live, and not hardly decent then."

GUINEAMEN

Mobjack Bay, Early November, 6:30 A.M.

Aboard the *Geneva K.* "This is a mean day today. Ain't no fit day to be working, I'll tell you that. No fit day to be working, not today it isn't." Gusts of wind whistled through the rigging and skittered across the water before mowing down the marsh grass. Jean King folded his collar close to his neck and backed away from the washboard to avoid the splash of a cresting wave. He smiled, then frowned, and said, "It's a shame's what it is. One of those mean days, that's all." There was a new moon in the early light, a starry sky, and a low mist over the marshes. King stood starboard aft at a stickup tiller and threaded the *Geneva K.* through marshes and oyster stakes on ruffled gray waters in a freshening southwesterly breeze, his destination Chesapeake Bay.

He fronted the wind with a linebacker's bulk and with no less presence. When he spoke, it was difficult to follow him—vowels clotted together in a fast-paced erratic sing-song that left little room for consonants or pauses. He compensated with repetition, varying his wording a little each time until at last his meaning was clear. The difficulty arose not from a defect in speech, but from a difference in language. Jean's was the language of Guinea Neck—the isolated marshlands had compressed his speech to a densely guttural patois unintelligible to outsiders, a dialect described by some as Devonshire English.

The southern rim of Mobjack Bay is an area as remote as it wild, a maze of marshes and fasts long isolated from the mainland, long accessible by sea, a desolate enclave that didn't see paved roads until after the Second World War. The area is called Guinea Neck, the people who live there Guineamen, or, somewhat disparagingly, Guinea Neckers.

Whatever their origins, Guineamen are held in a kind of awe by the people of the surrounding towns, a reverence intermingled with ignorance and fear.

How Guinea Neck came to be settled, and by whom, isn't known, which seems to be of much interest in the surrounding towns, where uncertainty finds expression in the form of legends. According to one legend about the settlement of Guinea Neck, British sailors, impressed into service from English bars and jails and rough neighborhoods—from the seedier sides of Bristol, of Plymouth, of Devonshire, England—came north to Guinea Neck after Cornwallis surrendered at Yorktown in 1781. The sailors are said to have stayed there to follow the water, never leaving out of fear of impressment or capture by pirates and privateers, for lack of brighter vistas. A marine scientist from the Virginia Institute of Marine Sciences Laboratory in Gloucester, Guinea Neck's nearest principal town, steeped as the scientists there are in the legends of Guinea Neck and perhaps not a little skeptical, stood one day at a train landing in Plymouth. An elderly man came ambling down the landing, recognized another man standing nearby and called out, " 'ey 'arry." As they began to speak there came from their mouths a fast-paced erratic sing-song that left little room for consonants or pauses.

Jim Haskett, historian of Yorktown's Colonial National Historic Park, has professional doubts about that view of the origin of Guinea Neck. He points out that the peninsula had been settled since the 1630s, that a fort had been erected in Gloucester as early as 1644 to protect the Colony's tobacco fleet from plundering pirates and privateers; and that, though the area was inaccessible by land, its accessibility by sea was what mattered then; and that the homogenizing influence of tidewater Colonial America was carried by sail.

On the other hand, Haskett says, his imagination engaging, there was a very large British hospital in Gloucester, and many of the King's men stayed on there to recuperate after the able-bodied prisoners of war were marched away. Haskett has seen a letter from the militia officer in charge of the hospital complaining to officers of the Continental Army that he didn't have enough manpower to guard the patients, that the King's men were wandering all over hell and back. British soldiers and sailors, a few Scotts and Germans, diffused outward through the Gloucester area, and the possibility remains, Haskett says, that some settled in the nearby marshes and became Guineamen. Haskett also points out, with increasing animation, that when British soldiers were impressed into service, when they reported for duty, they received a coin that may well have been a guinea. Perhaps the Guineamen found on the banks of the Chesapeake the riches promised by that coin, and so named their new home in its honor. Also within the realm of reasonable supposition, Haskett adds, is that a convict ship that broached in Mobjack Bay in the 1770s may have released Irish convicts to the surrounding marshes, convicts who may have then hid in the marshes and who became Guineamen.

Whatever their origins, Guineamen are held in a kind of awe by the people of the surrounding towns, a reverence intermingled with ignorance and fear. Guineamen are known locally for taking care of their own. It was a rare constable that would brave the marshes of Guinea Neck to get his man. "There's no law east of Tidemill," is a popular saying in Glouces-ter. Tidemill is the town just north of Gloucester, just west of Guinea Neck. Justice in Guinea Neck, it is said, was left to the Guineamen. If there was a killing, or some sort of problem, the families there would take care of it themselves. And, according to legend, in a field somewhere deep in the marshes of Guinea Neck, a field that could only be called Bloody Field, the bodies of those thus taken care of would be found, damp with the morning dew.

Transport and commerce along Guinea Neck traditionally centered on the water, and even today in large measure the Guineamen are watermen, the fishermen and crabbers and clammers of Mobjack Bay, of the lower Chesapeake, the oystermen of the York River. Jean King's forebears shared in this tradition on the water, as do Jean's brother and Jean himself, who works year round as a tonger for hard clams, *Mercenaria mercenaria.*

At 7:30 Jean throttled back the diesel and threw over the anchor—six fat steel links of chain the size of small footballs. The *Geneva K.* bobbed on the swells of the lower Chesapeake. It may as well have been the middle of the Atlantic—the Bay's eastern and western shores were shrouded in a low white mist that merged, imperceptively, with the gray sky, foreshortening the horizon to the length of the *Geneva K*. Jean went into the cabin to don his yellow bib. "About twenty-two, twenty-three feet here," he said coming out. "Twenty-three feet's what it is. I say we got twenty-three feet of water here." He unlashed his tongs from the culling board, walked back to the engine box, and pulled a lever that engaged the hauling mechanism (once the rear end of a Ford truck). To work it, Jean would step on a pedal that expanded brake shoes against a drum that would spin in response. Attached to the drum, where a tire had once turned, was a winch, whose line threaded up to the top of the boom, from which hung the tongs.

Jean stepped up to the culling board, a rectangular table on the cockpit's port side, forward of the engine box, put on his black rubber gloves and stepped on the pedal. The open tongs shot up two feet in the air, stopped, and began to free fall. Jean shoved them hard aport. They splashed into the water and dropped to the Bay floor. Again Jean pushed the pedal. The closed tongs erupted unseen from the Bay floor and shot through the water's surface, dripping with gray water. He removed his foot from the pedal, reached for the tongs, and guided them onto the culling board. Spreading the jaws, he set the drop hitch that would hold them open, pressed again on the pedal, and returned the tongs to the water. Left on the culling board were several fractured clumps of gray mud, which Jean rinsed away to reveal five hard clams.

A hole in a scrap of plywood two and one-half inches in diameter doubled or halved Jean's wages—the clams that fit through the opening were worth twice the ones that wouldn't. When it comes to hard clams, smaller is better—larger clams are tough, rubbery, fit only for grinding up for chowder and fetch only a nickel a piece. Smaller clams, called cherrystones or little necks, serve well as clams casino, or raw on the half shell, and fetch a dime. Jean tossed the smaller clams in a steel wire basket, leaving the larger ones scattered about a shelf of the culling board. At the end of the day he would load his clams, large and small, into separate burlap sacks ("CAFE MEXICANO," "CAFE DE EL SALVATOR"), from which they'd be taken and counted by the buyer. These clams, like the soft-shelled variety Tucker Brown harvests from the Potomac River, were destined mainly for New England, and for New York.

The next haul of the tongs came up with the same fractured mud and the same inadequate number of clams. "This is a mean day for clamming," Jean repeated. "I can't get nothing right on account of this haze—can't see no land this a way, no woods that a way. Mean day's what it is, I can tell you that." He couldn't tell where he was, much less where he wanted to be. Even so, he walked back to the stickup tiller and motored off into the haze, looking for a better spot, looking for more clams.

Hard clams have been caught around the Chesapeake as long as people have lived along its shores. The original, now recreational, way to catch them was to walk barefoot through nearshore waters and feel for clams with your feet. Monkeylike, you would grab a clam with your toes and slide it up the opposite leg. You would do this only in the southern Bay—hard clams can live only in the near-oceanic salinities of Virginia's Chesapeake.

Hand tongs (such as are used by Ben Waters and his brothers) were the first commercial gear pressed into service for the harvest of hard clams. Looking back from the 1980s, it's surprising that they worked—unlike oysters, which cement together on hard bottom, clams burrow individually in the sediment. One wouldn't expect, given today's standards, to find clams in sufficient density for such a small-volume method of harvest. By an earlier standard, one which lasted well into the 1950s, a set of hand tongs was all that was needed to harvest clams—so many were the clams, so densely clumped, they may as well have been stacked liked culled oysters. The horizon of Mobjack Bay was then dotted with clammers walking narrow washboards hauling up fractured clumps of gray mud crowded with clams.

Hand tongs had been first used to harvest oysters, and until late during the last century, the clammers and oystermen of the Chesapeake could either use them or they could dredge. There was only the one choice available, and for many it was no choice at all—getting a dredge rig together took a larger pile of money than many watermen would ever see. That left most watermen using tongs and, literally, risking their lives to harvest clams and oysters. In a review of the oyster industry in the 1887 Bureau of Fisheries Report, Ernest Ingersoll said: "Oyster-tonging involves great exposure, hard labor, and some risk, and the men engaged in it are mostly adult males in the vigor of health. The injury to health from exposure is so great that few ever reach old age. The death rate among oystermen, as compared with other trades, is very great."

The hardships of the oystermen were shared by the clammers, many of whom also worked through winter. In addition to the exposure and the physical hardship, hand tongers were constrained by the depths they were able to work. It was a rare waterman who could wield tongs over twenty-eight feet, and many of the Chesapeake's oyster beds were below thirty. The shallow water beds were the first picked clean, and were the only beds the hand tongers could work. For clammers, a constraint in using hand tongs emerged and grew and grew in proportion as the clam bottoms thinned—as more and more clams were taken from the mud, as fewer and fewer clams were left behind, the small scoop taken by a pair of hand tongs became too small for reasonable harvest.

That left most watermen using tongs and, literally, risking their lives to harvest clams and oysters.

An answer to the problem of declining oysters and thinning clams was patented in Virginia in 1890 by Joseph A. Bristow and William M. Dixon, and again in Maryland in 1891 by James B. Tawes, as "Oyster-Tongs." Tawes, the father of Maryland's former Governor J. Millard Tawes, in his patent application, stated: "This invention related to oyster-tongs, and has for its object to improve the general construction of the same, whereby the efficiency of this class of devices is increased and the same rendered more convenient to operate."

Physically, the invention stripped the hand tongs of their shafts, replacing them with steel levers. Their baskets were lengthened, their weight increased, and a drop hitch was attached to the levers to keep them open. When the tongs hit the Bay floor the drop hitch swung clear, enabling the tongs to close when hauled by their line to the surface.

The effect of these changes was to increase, dramatically, the tongs' efficiency. Patent tongs, as they came to be called, could now haul much larger loads than one man could former-ly dead lift. And because the tongs were so much larger, the area of ground scooped with each haul held more clams. Lifted by winder, usually a log with crank attached, the patent tongs offered a further advantage in that oyster bars and clam bottoms of any depth, bottoms formerly available only to the dredge, became accessible to the tong.

The evolution of tongs took another large step forward when, in the 1920s, cheap and reliable gasoline engines first came to the water. The Chesapeake's sailing fleets exchanged their sails and masts for motors, the patent tongers their hand winders for power.

Jean throttled back the diesel, pulled the wire that actuated the winch and walked up to his culling board. He looked out over the water, and said, "You ain't got a very good day is what I can tell you. Breezing up all the time. I say, breezing up all the time now. I say most in the west. I say twenty mile or more. Actually, you ain't got much of a day, no sir." He stepped on the pedal. The first lick had three clams and one moon snail. Moon snails prey on clams. Using a rasp-like tongue called a radula, they bore through the clam shell and suck out the soft flesh. "I can't throw these over where I work," Jean said. "No sir."

Jean took two more licks, and then again dragged anchor to look elsewhere. The miles he had come to tong clams and the meagerness of his harvest were expressions of two problems now familiar to the Chesapeake. The first problem was overfishing. As was the case with oysters in the last century, and in the early years of this one, too many clams were taken, too many boats bobbed over the clam beds of Mobjack Bay. And compounding the overfishing was the decreasing recruitment of young clams—fewer clams attained adulthood, fewer clams burrowed into the sediment. The reason was that other, newer, problem facing the Chesapeake—too many nutrients. To the right side of the formula that read too many nutrients equals not enough light (and not enough grasses) could now be added not enough clams.

Dexter Haven, a marine biologist now retired from the Virginia Institute of Marine Sciences, had begun working on the Bay in 1949, and in 1953 moved with the laboratory to Gloucester Point. For over thirty years he worked with the Guineamen, tagging their fish as they came off the boat, taking scale samples. The Guineamen accorded Haven the sort of beneficent attention usually reserved for the mentally deficient. "It was never that anybody was hostile or antagonistic," Haven says. "Far from it. They might have thought we were a bunch of eggheads, and we probably were." Dexter Haven has watched the Guineamen and the waters of the Chesapeake all those years, and in his observations there is reason for uneasy reflection.

"What happened to clamming," Haven says, "is they were overfished, and the eelgrass, which used to be a good habitat for the clams to get established in, has all disappeared. I don't think that's the whole answer, but it's a big part of it. Eelgrass beds were habitat that protected clams from predation by blue crabs, and provided a site for the hard clam to attach. The clam, during the first week after it goes through larval stage, forms a little thread-like thing called a byssal thread that it attaches to some firm object like a frond of eelgrass. Then it drops off and goes into the bottom. There used to be tremendous quantities of eelgrass around the margin of Mobjack Bay and the mouth of York river. Eelgrass was almost everywhere during the forties and fifties, but it's all gone now, and this loss of the eelgrass in the lower Bay is a major reason for a decline in the clam fishery in the shallow water. Back in the days of the Guineamen, back in the 1940s and '50s, there were so many hard clams you could get them with the hand tongs. You'd go in shallow water. I think I saw my last hand tonger for clams in the Bay about six years ago. Now, there aren't enough hard clams in shallow water so a man can make a living at it."

Like the widening ripples from a pebble thrown into a clear pond, too many nutrients had caused a widening circle of problems, had led to the paucity of clams. And the story didn't end there—the loss or decline of one species leads to the deplenishment of others. When a species declines, watermen don't put away their gear and move into executive suites, they switch to other species to harvest; a fairly constant number of watermen converge on fewer species.

Haven continues: "The Guineamen were watermen. They'd follow the water. You had all different kinds of fisheries back then. You had the gill net fishery, mainly in the summertime. Then you'd have the stake gill net fishery; that would be late winter, early in spring, and that would be for the shad and the striped bass. Then that would sort of die down. There were pound net fisheries from April, May, June, July, August and September. Then that would die down.

And in the summer, if you weren't fishing pound nets, you were fishing crab pots. You could also clam the year round. The thing about the watermen back in the days of the Guineamen, one could go home and decide, "Well, I think I'll go clam for two or three weeks," and he'd clam for two or three weeks, and then he might go out and get a few oysters and sell them to a dealer. In other words, he wasn't tied down to any one of those fisheries. If the one in front of his house wasn't very good one year, he could do something else. He'd be putting pots out that year, or he might decide to work in the James River that year to get some seed oysters to be planted, to be sold to the leaseholders to be planted on their private grounds. He wasn't really tied down to anything. The way things are now, there's not enough to go around, certainly with the oysters, and the watermen are left concentrating on what's left."

That concentrating heightens the pressure on the numbers and kinds of animals that are left. And sometimes the concentrating leads to tensions among the watermen who fish them.

Back aboard the *Geneva K.*, at noon, Jean King was about ready to call it a day. "This ain't no clams, long as I been working here. You can't catch no clams this kind of weather. It's a shame. One of those mean days, that's all. I'll call it a day. I ain't catching nothing. Call it a day. You get these kind of days out here. This is open water here. This isn't no Mobjack Bay. This is the Chesapeake, this is."

For the day, he had harvested eight hundred clams, a hundred of them large. He hauled his anchor, went into the cabin, and came out with a small stool he placed beside his stickup tiller. He took a Diet-Rite out of an ice chest under the culling board, sat on his stool, and turned the *Geneva K.* northwest, toward Mobjack Bay.

"What do you think of this for a living?" he said. "I reckon I'll stick with it. I'm too old to do anything else now, I reckon. I say I'll stick with it."

CHOPTANK SELECTS

Knapps Narrows, January, 5:00 A.M.

Knapps Narrows, a tide-ripped watercourse joining the Choptank River to the open Bay, separates Tilghman Island from Maryland's Eastern Shore. Over its waters, red, green and white lights darted about erratically like multicolored fireflies, marking by their presence unseen workboats jockeying about the swift tidal current waiting to pass beneath the bascule bridge that spans the Narrows. Hand tongers headed east, toward the lower reaches of the Choptank River, as did most dredge boats. Patent tongers headed west, toward the open Bay.

"That's a puff."

This morning a puff was a gust of wind topping twenty-five knots. It could blow the feathery tops of reed grasses over to an angle of thirty degrees. A puff could push workboats hard against docking lines and cause them to creak in response, cause pilings to groan. A puff whipped through the open-windowed cab of Aldon Lednum's Ford pickup, where it registered as needles in the face. In the face of a puff, the National Weather Service forecast is quickly forgotten. A puff means stay in the harbor.

Aldon patent tongs. He keeps the *Retriever* in a slip along the Bay side of the Narrows, where its creaks and groans now traveled the wind, now registered in the cab of his Ford pickup. Knapps Narrows has a bellwether in Robby Wilson, captain and owner of the skipjack *Ellsworth*. When Robby stays in everyone stays in. This morning Robby was out. Decision hung in the wind. It's two hours before sunrise and two degrees below freezing. Aldon, his Ford idling, the heater blasting, pointed his face through the open window, his hair blowing in the wind. Jerry and Chester, pulled up alongside in Jerry's Ford pickup, their windows open, their heater blasting, counted the puffs and searched each other's faces. Uncertainty swirled like an eddy.

A prolonged, puffless calm made the decision go.

Clear of the Narrows, Aldon motored the *Retriever* through large rollers. Jerry and Chester followed two hundred yards astern, the *Miss Cindy* in silhouette against the ruddy eastern horizon, her running lights unlit. Aldon and Jerry leave and return together, often separating during the day, and today Aldon would go farther down the Bay than Jerry and Chester would follow. As the *Retriever* turned south, *Miss Cindy* merged into the northern darkness.

Aldon is a Marlboro man, literally as well as figuratively. After a day on the water, his flip-top box will be half empty. To look at him is to see roadside billboards come to life. In his erect carriage and natural reticence is the suggestion of serious purpose. His chiseled features, weathered bright red, were fixed in a sea of wavy brown hair that spilled from his baseball cap and swept down his cheeks in porkchop sideburns to meet in a mustache. In his dark blue Sears snowsuit and black rubber boots, he looked poised for an encounter with a polar bear. He spoke slowly, his voice incubating momentarily somewhere deep in his chest before issuing forth in deliberate tones that rose and fell unpredictably on syllables variously elongated or clipped. In the Aldon Lednum lexicon "Ford" is a two-syllable word.

Perched high on a bucket seat in the *Retriever*'s cabin, Aldon, unaccustomed to the barrier, strained to see through the wave-washed glass. His preferred helm was just aft of the culling board in the open cockpit, and now, as he looked back over his left shoulder to check on his position, a puff picked up a wave crest and dropped it squarely on the board, where it scattered like bomb rubble, the aft cockpit momentarily lost at sea. Jimmy, his stepfather, twenty miles down Bay, hailed on the VHF:

"You got a weather report for tomorrow?"

"The man gives a bad report—wind gusts to forty."

"Hell, that ain't too bad given what we've had lately. If it does what the man says, I'll go ahead and put a set of inserts in her."

"If it's blowing a gale, I'll come down."

"I could use a torque wrench if you got one."

"Uh huh. Yeah, they're calling for all kind of good stuff tomorrow—northeast coming southeast."

"If it's raining I won't mind it much. If it's pouring you can't get nothing right."

A rogue roller washed up the windshield and over the cabin top, arcing onto the aft cockpit. Aldon lit his first cigarette of the day, exhaling a long, forced breath into the microphone. "Everything I got is tired this morning. And the closer I get to those shells the tireder I get."

"That's one thing about bad bearings—you can't run her hard. I got an excuse not to hurry. Yeah, I got out of practice. I'm over the hill now. On the downgrade."

"You got a long ways yet."

"Yeah, if you call fifteen years a long ways. I guess it is if I got to do this the rest of my life."

Jerry was listening in on this conversation but, because his aerial was broken, could hear only Aldon's side of it. He continually interrupted, asking Aldon to repeat the other half of the conversation, prompting Jimmy to quip:

"Let's take a collection and get him an aerial."

"He'll be alright when he gets his new boat."

"No, he won't see out of the windows of that boat."

"Is he making fun at me, Aldon?"

"Yeah, if you call fifteen years a long ways. I guess it is if I got to do this the rest of my life."

~⌒~

6:00 A.M. Propelled by a hydraulic takeoff backed by three-hundred-and-fifty Chevy horsepower, Aldon's tongs burst through the water and slapped back—once, twice, three times, before he hauled them above the culling board. Aldon was perched just aft of the board along the starboard gunwale, face to the wind, dancing on the hydraulic pedals like an organ player at a revival meeting, his legs absorbing and balancing the *Retriever*'s rising and plummeting bronco-like ride on the rollers of the open Bay.

Balanced between wind and tide, not using an anchor, the *Retriever* bucked and dived. Ten feet below her keel lay the Diamonds, the oyster bar between Sharps Island lighthouse and Falls Channel, an uncharted, boulder-strewn submarine gully parallel to the main shipping lane midway up the Chesapeake's eastern rim. The northerly winds, which had lightened to a steady fifteen knots, pushed against the flooding tide. The two held the *Retriever* in latitudinal equilibrium, and Aldon in altitudinal flux.

Patent tongs such as Aldon's were first used around 1963 or 1964. It was then that Larry Simns, a waterman who now also presides over the Maryland Watermen's Association, saw a patent tong rig in Solomons Island powered by hydraulic motor. Larry noticed that by using hydraulics the tongs could be held suspended in the air at any height, and that their rate and moment of descent could be carefully controlled. He had a particular interest in these improvements, having spent six months the previous year hospitalized, his face stove in by the long lever of a patent tong in free fall. The rig Larry saw in Solomons was manipulated by hand controls and worked awkwardly. Larry's insight was to fashion pedals, thus freeing his hands for the tongs. And because the tongs could be opened as well as closed by hydraulics, there was no longer a need for a drop hitch, or for such dangerously long levers. A further advantage was that the number of licks one could take increased from one per minute to three.

Aldon reached for the tongs and swung them over the culling board, where he opened the teeth to spill his catch. It took thirty-three seconds from the time the tongs emerged from the water until they were returned to it, a half-minute requiring two feet, two hands and a healthy set of pectorals.

First, Aldon stepped on the left pedal to close the tongs, forcing its jaws into the oyster bar below. He then pressed the right pedal to actuate the hydraulic motor that hauled them up. The motor revved in response, rattling a plywood casing that amplified the motor's roar and added its own reverberations. Curbside, Indy 500.

When the tongs were chest high Aldon leaned out over the water and grabbed them. He swung them toward the culling board, and just as they reached the apogee of their swing, he jammed down on the left pedal to open them and spill the catch. He shoved the tongs back over the water and shifted a foot onto the right pedal to drop them. "The only thing tired in this job is your feet," he said.

As the tongs fell, Aldon culled the catch, throwing the oysters ahead of him onto the mound on the cockpit sole. He paused, drew deep from a Pepsi, and pitched the empty overboard. Then he swept the cull overboard as well, and cupped his gloved hands over the *Retriever*'s upright exhaust.

The *Retriever* measured forty-two feet by eleven. Her lines were rakish. There was eagerness in her low-slung sheer and upward-sweeping bow and poise in her fine cut through the water. She didn't pound in rolling seas, as do many flat-bottomed Chesapeake workboats, but bounded gracefully from roller to roller in a light frolic. Like her captain, she was organized and neat and, except for her varnished transom, without frills. And smart—also unlike many Chesapeake workboats, the *Retriever* was equipped with life preservers and even a rudimentary first aid kit. Aldon, himself not entirely without frills, as the tattooed purple star on his neck attested ("We was all just out of high school," he said, "bamboozling around."), checked her papers to see that she was built in 1946. Bronza Parks, known to watermen throughout the Bay for his keen eye for a graceful line, built her, Aldon said, when he was an old man. (Bronza never did get too old— after many successful years building workboats, he took to building yachts; a dissatisfied suburban client argued Bronza to an early death with a pistol.)

Local custom on Tilghman Island centers on working the Chesapeake's waters. The islanders catch and sell, buy and ship, or simply serve Chesapeake Bay seafood, as they have for generations, ever since Matthew Tilghman bought the island in 1741. Measuring three miles by one, the island dangles from the finger of a meandering arm of the middle Eastern Shore. Its small community, which had traditionally resisted the cosmopolitan influences of nearby Washington, D.C., Baltimore and Annapolis, was changing now as out-of-town money increasingly appeared in the form of resort homes and pleasure yachts and higher property values. These changes are not welcomed by everyone without reservation. Recently, Wadey Murphy, trotliner and skipjack captain, walked with his son along one of Tilghman's many points, an area he and his forebears had always walked. To his way of thinking—and according to local custom—the point had always been titled but the shoreline never owned. A new owner, fresh from Washington, D.C., kicked him off.

Generally, if you get a bad season for oysters, marketwise, then it's rough on crabbing.

Aldon had less cause to resent out-of-town influences than many natives—he met his wife Kim one summer while her family vacationed in their Tilghman Island summer home. Change to Aldon registered mainly on the shoreline, where familiar landmarks and early morning lights changed too often for memory, making the coastline unknowable, his piloting confusing. His next boat, Aldon vowed, would have radar, on whose flickering green screen the image of islands and points would offer an unvarying picture.

Aldon knows the Lednum family picture two generations back. His grandfather ran fishing parties; his father and stepfather work locally as watermen, as do his many brothers and cousins. Beyond that, the Lednum ancestry is seemingly unknown to Aldon.

More than two-and-a-half centuries ago, in 1720, Edward Ledenham came as a sailor to Broad Creek Neck, a ragged marshy peninsula from the mainland two miles east of Tilghman Island. Settling there with his wife Bridgette, he took up land trades. Together the Ledenhams raised an Edward, a Nathaniel, free males of Talbot County. From them came Lednums, as the name became in 1850, in fair numbers, Lednums who would hang close to local shores, who would work the water, leaving only to serve when called—first in the Broad Creek Militia during the Revolution, later as Loyalists during the War of 1812, later still as Union supporters.

A woman from the South recently sent Aldon a letter inquiring about the family. The postmark read Louisiana and the return address bore the surname Lednum in a decidedly feminine hand. Also a Lednum, she wanted to trace the family genealogy, and promised to share her researches. When the letter arrived, Aldon was on the Bay. Kim worried over it most of the day. Later she said to Aldon: "I thought you told me you never married before."

"You want to keep a happy home down here you don't fool around," Aldon counseled as he culled his catch. "They know before you do."

Aldon dropped the tongs to the Bay floor and hauled back. In the load was a loose matrix of shells and oysters—only a few were living, many had recently died, most were blackened and smoothed from years swept by sediments. In among the shells and oysters was a female crab, which appeared neither living nor dead but somewhere between, roused but slightly from her winter-long hibernation. Aldon tossed her into a basket with others.

"This cold water has put a hurting on them," he said as he watched them for signs of life. "Most of your males will stay away from the females when they're buried. I don't know where the males are this year—I imagine they're off buried deep." In another haul of the tongs came two more females, one too small to keep. The larger he placed on the culling board, where he pulled at her claws and jerked at her swimmerets. Dead. Throwing her overboard, he went on, "Yeah, this kind of weather puts me in the mood for crabbing. Generally, if you get a bad season for oysters, marketwise, then it's rough on crabbing. Nobody's spending any money. It's the common working man eats seafood. None of your rich people do. Last year we was tickled to get seven bushels of oysters but of course we got twenty dollars a bushel for them. This year I get my limit most the time but can't get more than fourteen. They'll be a mess a crabs here come summertime, I'll tell you that."

Even now, in wind-tossed, steely gray wintry waters, the prodigious Chesapeake productivity was much in evidence. Over the culling board passed skilletfish, toadfish and gobies. Worms and clams and crabs—several varieties each. Shrimp and mussels and sponges variously attached to shells and stones (and empties from six-ounce Pepsi's). Oysters three years from harvest among barnacles and blennies. A delirium of life, in this one spot no larger than the width of Aldon's tongs.

He had come to this on evidence of the telescanner depth recorder, on whose wavy-lined, continuous-readout CRT screen the practiced eye can discern changes in the depth and texture of the bottom; on evidence, too, of the tactile twitch of a thin nylon cord, to the nether end of which was tied three feet of chain. Aldon slowly motored the *Retriever* as he held the line in his outstretched left arm, and as the chain dragged along the bottom he sensed through its twitch the texture of mud or sand or oysters. The line quivered, then vibrated, then translated the tight, staccato jerks that promised oyster bar. Glancing up and forward at the telescan for confirmation, he saw smooth bottom. "This must be a clay slab or stone or something," he said, stopping nevertheless to drop his tongs to test it. "All it would take is one little spot—I've pulled my limit off spots smaller than that culling board."

Aldon generally gets his limit. Some oystermen, deterred by the wind, by the market, by a layer of skim ice that would not obstruct a duck, ride it out in open-windowed pickup trucks in early morning light and then leave for home. Others venture out to try their luck and then leave for port—as two boats steaming from the south now did—on the heels of the wind. Aldon said, "You got to have a lot of patience this time of year. I usually stick it out unless its blowing a gale or I can't hit nothing."

The catch so far was nothing much, by Aldon's reckoning, but what oysters he caught looked far nicer than those hauled from the Nanticoke, larger and fatter. They were also free of the oozing green mud that lines the bottoms of most Eastern Shore tributary rivers. Covered in patches of bright orange bryozoans, they resembled clowns. The salinity of the water accounted for the difference; oysters grow faster and fatter in the more saline waters of the open Bay. The difference is one you can savor—open Bay oysters taste saltier and have a faint aroma of iodine.

Like a flow-through filter, an oyster absorbs chemicals from the water, good and bad, chemicals which impart to it a regional flavor, a remembrance of the waters from which it came.

The blue point oyster of Brookhaven Bay, New York, was thought to be of such delicate flavor and succulent texture that the English imported them by the freighterful as gourmet fare. The Chincoteagues and Lynn Havens of Virginia have long been praised here and abroad for their saltiness. The difference is not the oyster (they're all American oysters, *Crassostrea virginica*) but the water. Chincoteagues and Lynn Havens, in fact, were usually James River oysters transplanted there to depurate, to pump local, more saline waters through their mantles at the rate of seven gallons per hour. The regional flavoring that sent Englishmen plunging deep into their wallets and far onto the sea is evident even in oysters taken from bars in close proximity. To the practiced palate, an oyster taken by a Choptank River hand tonger is a different animal from those Aldon took in the open Bay, as he would readily tell you.

Like a flow-through filter, an oyster absorbs chemicals from the water, good and bad.

The distinction most important to shucking houses, and to Aldon, is how the oysters were caught. Hand tongers, who usually work the tributary rivers, often have trouble finding a buyer for their smaller oysters. Some buyers, Aldon had heard, had been loading their trucks mostly with hand-tonged oysters only to fill in the back with those taken by patent tong just so a shucking house would accept them.

To Aldon's way of thinking, the oysters he was catching were selects, in the scale of standards, selects and extra selects. This may have been wishful thinking. Selects usually go one hundred and fifty to a bushel, and his catch, so far, went about twice that, placing them squarely in the standard zone. They would go selects, he figured, because they were fatter than the usual standard, but also because no one else was catching selects. The terms are not fixed, sliding from year to year, or even month to month, relative to what oysters are available. Aldon is known to care about the quality of his catch and usually brings in the best. Years ago Aldon and his brother worked oyster beds with twenty-eight-foot hand tongs in the open Bay. When those deep-water beds gave out he switched to patent tongs, never pausing to try his luck with shorter tongs on the nearby Choptank River. "Your river oyster ain't nothing like as fat and pretty as your Bay oyster," he said, and he won't fiddle with them. His buyer, knowing all this, may well allow some slack in the definition of select.

The telescanner had told it true. Thick slabs of compacted, clayey mud came up in the tongs—but no oysters. "I'll get lucky in a minute," Aldon said. "Wouldn't take much—back when oysters was thick I pulled a hundred-ten bushels in an hour's time. Just one teeny little spot is all it'd take."

~⌒

"Your river oyster ain't nothing like as fat and pretty as your Bay oyster."

Falls Channel, 2:00 P.M., held firm in a stiffening breeze and ebbing tide by drag weights, two automobile crankshafts tied together with nylon cord and cleated to the stern. The *Retriever* rollercoastered over breaking waves—now in a trough, now on a crest, now lunging between. The sky was unrelievedly gray. Aldon's earlier foray onto the Diamonds hadn't panned out and he had now reluctantly joined several other Tilghman Island patent tongers—the *Moonraker*, *Stardust* and *Joker* among them—already working Falls Channel. The oysters here are smaller, the bottom harder on the gear.

Aldon dropped his tongs to the Bay floor and hauled back, sending the *Retriever* into an uncharacteristic windward, crossways lurch. Oysters here attach to boulders the size of ice chests. He broke the conglomerate free with his gloved fists, hacking at one particularly tenacious oyster for several seconds without effect before knocking it against the culling board. When it still wouldn't give, he grabbed a claw hammer from the engine box and broke its shell. He smiled sheepishly and threw it onto the mound with the rest. The boulder he threw overboard, causing a splash that the wind carried to his face, deepening his smile. Sometimes the boulders broke the teeth of the tongs. Noticing another lost tooth, Aldon grimaced, and said, "I'm going to have to put a partial plate in her if I keep this up."

Aldon's tongs were uncharacteristically large, six feet wide at their mouths as opposed to the usual four or five. As with most things on Aldon's boat, he had built them himself. "With these tongs," he said with apparent pride, "you can catch your limit most any day."

The hauls came up quickly. The ratio of oysters to boulders hovered at three to one. Sometimes it climbed to double digits, and at these moments Aldon dog paddled and smiled his way through the cull as his feet danced on the hydraulic pedals.

Miss Cindy bore down on the *Retriever* from the northwest, tracking a threatening course of uncertain intent. Seconds before impact, Jerry backed her off with an authoritative reverse thrust. Manifesting nonchalance, he surveyed the pyramidal mound on the *Retriever*'s cockpit sole and shouted, "Hey Aldon, those look like Choptank Selects." Aldon smiled broadly, threw a smaller-than-usual oyster onto the mound and dropped his tongs to the Bay floor. They were small, yes, but they hadn't come from no river.

In deepening twilight, the breeze commenced to blow a gale. Aldon culled out the few remaining oysters from the culling board, dropped his tongs to the Bay floor and hauled up the drag weights. He turned east, *Miss Cindy* two hundred yards astern in silhouette in the twilight western horizon.

This was no lazy backwater, no floodplain river shouldered in by headlands and sheltered by trees from the wind. This was open Bay. Out here a northerly breeze has a hundred-mile fetch to gain momentum and declare its intentions. Winds here don't buffet so much as molest, driving the near-freezing spray scoured from the waves horizontally into Aldon's face.

Aldon turned up his snowsuit collar, pulled his brim low and slid a shovel into the mound of oysters. He paused to take the last draw from his Pepsi and then pitched the empty overboard. The oysters he folded into bushel baskets like a fine batter, pausing after each basket to sculpt its top with a few well-placed shells, his point being to get a little air in there, to stretch the catch to the twenty-five-bushel limit.

A puff picked up a wave crest and slammed it hard onto stacked baskets of Chesapeake Bay Selects. Small rivulets of tawny water drained from their sides and bottoms onto the plywood cockpit sole where they mixed with wave wash and poured into the bilge. "It can blow now, we can go home."

Aldon Lednum smiled, his face into the wind. "Just think," he added. "I get to come and do this all over again tomorrow."

CHANCE

Northern Tangier Sound, February, 5:30 A.M.

The foresail luffed, then billowed, then filled with a light northeasterly breeze. The *Helen Virginia* heeled, lurched tentatively forward, and then surged.

"Go wind'ard."

Over the roller flew the windward dredge, into the clear green waters of Tangier Sound. Forty feet of steel cable payed out from the starboard drum of the winder and snapped taut against the becket. Dredge teeth dug into oyster bar. The *Helen Virginia* heeled low in the water and slowed.

Skipper Jack Parkinson grabbed a thin line off the hatch cover and yanked it, causing a stutter, then a roar in the donkey engine, signaling Butch to turn the lever that engages the winder drum. Up came the windward dredge, slowly through the water's surface, hard against the horizontal roller. Grasping large steel rings hanging from the back of the dredge's net bag, Jackie and Steve heaved the catch onto the deck. They dropped to their knees, to rough-sawn oak planks now wet with splash and slippery with mud and culled the catch. Thirty-seven oysters, one blue crab, a bushel of red moss and shells. The oysters were thrown forward or aft onto the pine-plank deck covering. The blue crab, red moss and shells were shoveled into water made turbid and brown.

The *Helen Virginia* came about; again, her foresail luffed, billowed out, and then filled with a now freshening northeasterly breeze.

"Go."

Over the rollers sailed the windward and leeward dredges, into the oyster bar that for miles around lined the bottom of northern Tangier Sound. Butch and Barry sat on the winder cables, feeling the vibration imparted by the jerky drag of dredge on oyster bottom, gauging through their haunches how large would be the catch, how fat their wallets.

It was Steve who first noticed the cabin cruiser bearing down from the east, planing on the water, kicking up considerable spray. "Man, that bitch come by wide open."

Jack scanned the pink and gray horizon for the familiar silhouette. "They don't generally come out this early—trying to catch somebody doing something I guess."

The vessel, named the *West River* and registered to the Maryland Marine Police, came within hailing distance. What she would catch, apparently, was the *Helen Virginia*. Throttling back, the *West River* hung hard aport, within yards of the *Helen Virginia*'s reaching boom, and circled.

"Five bucks and I'll drop my drawers."

"I got five says you won't."

Off came the Grundens of Herkules foul-weather parka. Down came the bib. The pants. The longjohns. Into the wind shot the pale moon, into the faces of the Maryland Marine Police, waterborne escort for a photographer who would catch on film the *Helen Virginia*, one of thirty-odd skipjacks composing the nation's last commercial sailing fleet.

Jack turned away from the *West River* to hide his broad grin. He cupped his hands and lit a Muriel Air Tip. The smoke hung in the wind like white laughter.

Ranging in age from seven years to over one hundred, Chesapeake Bay skipjacks sail only from Maryland, mainly from Tilghman or Deal islands, always to familiar oyster bars and an uncertain future. They are graceful and swift under press of canvas, evoking from a distance a serene sense of timelessness and calm. They are also teetering on the brink of extinction, preserved only through inefficiencies legislated by a populace enchanted with dredge boats under sail and fearful of the power of the mechanized dredge.

The history of Chesapeake oyster dredging may well engender fear, punctuated as it is by over-harvesting, kidnapping and murder. It began in the 1820s in New England, when oyster beds in Connecticut, Long Island and Cape Cod became decimated by the indiscriminate use of the dredge. A triangular steel frame supporting a rope-and-chain net bag, the dredge is the most efficient gear ever developed for harvesting oysters. When dragged along the bottom, a forty-four-inch swath (forty-two for hard-bottom dredges) of oyster bar is scooped through its jaws

and swept into its bag, which may take upwards of three hundred pounds of oysters and shell with every lick. Take too many licks and you shave the bar back to bare bottom. Too many licks were taken in New England early during the last century, prompting the entrepreneurial New Englanders to swarm south. From sloops and schooners they threw over their dredges to scoop the floor of Chesapeake Bay.

Angry Marylanders first passed laws forbid-

A triangular steel frame supporting a rope-and-chain net bag, the dredge is the most efficient gear ever developed for harvesting oysters.

ding the use of the dredge, then accommodated it, and then passed laws sanctioning it—laws which stipulated that only Marylanders could dredge. Yankees then packed their belongings and moved south, becoming Marylanders in their migration, and dredged the length and breadth of the Bay. Deep submarine hills hard and high with oysters were shaved bare, left low and soft. They dredged deeper water beds first, beds their blue-water keelboats could easily traverse, and when they scraped those clean, Marylanders, both new and native, developed shallow craft that could sail shoal waters. They made them faster and cheaper, and they made them quickly—an oyster boom was on and no one wanted to be left at the dock. First was the bugeye, the name perhaps derived from the Scotch "buckie," meaning oyster shell and applied to a Scottish boat of similar profile. Then the skipjack, so named for a fish that skitters across the Chesapeake's surface. Locally known as a "drudge boat," the skipjack is now honored as the Maryland State Boat.

All this for oysters. Oysters that went to Philadelphia parlors and Colorado ranches, to California miners and English noblemen.

"A lot of folks photograph these boats," said Jack, still grinning, his hands on the wheel, piloting a course that took full advantage of a sailing vessel's right-of-way, forcing the *West River* further abeam than her photographer might like. He grabbed the throttle cord off the deck and pulled; the donkey engine noised up, signaling the crew to engage the levers to haul the dredges. The leeward dredge came up askew, its side to the roller. Danny-Ray jabbed a two-by-four into the dredge's steel frame, and flipped it over.

Originally dredges were hauled by hand winder, with four men to a winder and, typically, two winders to a boat. The job paid little and was literally back breaking—a free-wheeling winder could throw a man into the sea with a cracked spine. Knowledgeable natives avoided a turn at the winder, if possible: a shortage of labor was commonplace. And here the history of dredging reached a Dark Age. Foreigners, Germans and Irish, and blacks were shanghaied from Baltimore waterfront bars and taverns and forced to work winders on drudge boats that for weeks didn't see port, for captains who kept them locked in the cabin. At the end of a season, a crew thus imprisoned might be found floating down-Bay, paid off with the boom—called onto deck as the captain steered hard to force the boom swinging at their heads.

All this for oysters. Oysters that went to Philadelphia parlors and Colorado ranches, to California miners and English noblemen. Chesapeake oysters to supply a hungry demand that had left the oyster beds of Great Britain and the continent, of New England, decimated beyond revival.

Oyster dredging and commerce continued with ever greater intensity well into the 1860s, interrupted then only by transportation and market problems brought on by hostilities farther west—the Civil War. Union-supporting Deal Island harbored seventy skipjacks then, most of whose captains scrambled for whatever money they could make, many of whom ran blockades not for the Union but for the Confederates.

After the war, dredging intensified anew, spurred by a law legalizing use of the dredge, and by the promise of fifty dollars a bushel—a hundred times the prevailing Chesapeake price, from London buyers. Maryland oystermen scrambled onto the Bay, pushing the harvests up to fifteen million bushels in 1885, seven times higher than the average catch of recent years, higher than they would ever go again.

Often the scramble deteriorated into skirmishes between dredgers and tongers. Oystermen who didn't dredge tonged, and the tongers were more in number and greater in political importance. At their behest, the law that permitted dredging forbade drudge boats from entering the rich shallows of the tributary rivers. But drudge boat captains violated the regulations en masse, prompting, in their dramatic disobedience, the formation of the Maryland Oyster Navy. Tongers and dredgers fought it out with carbines and cannon, the Oyster Navy running interference with bow-mounted howitzers, drawing fire from both sides. Hostilities eventually ended, mainly because catches declined to the point where they weren't worth dying for and because another war would interrupt commerce and be followed by economic depression, not to mention the increasing size and effectiveness of the Oyster Navy, which would later become the Maryland Marine Police.

The antipathy of watermen to the Marine Police is mainly gone now, its residual emotions deeply subsurface. Left in its place is a grudging respect commingled, at times, with irreverence.

"You can keep that five, cap—it was worth it just to see their faces."

The day started breezeless and dark, February's full moon radiating unseen above wispy cirrus clouds, and subfreezing damp cold. The *Helen Virginia*'s crew sat huddled in three idling pickups on the oyster shell lot adjoining the Last Chance Marina ("CAFE-BAR, FAMILY DINING & ENTERTAINMENT") on Deal Island, Maryland, waiting for Jack, who—across the bridge in Don's Hardware Store—drank coffee and chatted it up around the gas heater, talking to other drudge boat captains about the weather, the price of oysters, the day to come.

"They's catching more oysters down the Sound though they's small," Jack said to his assembled crew as he pulled up. "And we won't need much wind down that way. Let's try her out." With that he hopped back in his truck and drove across the lot to a bulkhead and the *Helen Virginia*. Butch, Barry, Steve and Danny-Ray, sons and father Thomases, Thomas (*not a Thomas*), and Jack's son Jackie climbed down from their pickups and ambled over.

The *Helen Virginia* sat low in the water. One tall mast, stepped just forward of the cabin and raking aft, supported a boom drooping under the weight of rolled metal patches. Her dredge rollers were deeply grooved; her metalwork, flaked with rust, hung loose on worried fastenings.

The same law that enabled the use of the dredge proscribed its use in boats having a means of self-propulsion other than sails. More recent legislation continued this prohibition but also allowed, on Mondays and Tuesdays, dredging under power. The answer to these seemingly contradictory regulations is the yawl boat, three hundred and fifty horsepower of engine, typically General Motors, encased in a twelve-foot hull that on sailing days hangs in the breeze, suspended off the stern from davits, in easy view of the Maryland Marine Police, and on power days pushes skipjacks like barges over oyster bars. Yawl boats may also be used to power the skipjacks out to the beds, a practice followed by most skippers, except in the stiffest of breezes.

Butch climbed back into the yawl boat and started her, as the rest of the crew came aft from the foredeck to man the lines that would lower her into the water.

"Come on ahead on her. Come on ahead on her, Butch. Take your time now or you'll be overboard. All right, slow her down, put her in the chock." Turning in her own length, the *Helen Virginia* was pushed passed a sandspit hairy with reed grasses, past a stone jetty and out into Tangier Sound. She came, in her broad turn, within jousting distance of a patent tonger. With practiced indifference, her captain muscled up on the throttle, narrowly averting collision. "I did hit a patent tonger once," Jack said. "You see they drift with the tide and I can't move around as well as they, especially under sail. I broke a line and her running lights is all."

The *Helen Virginia*, together with other Deal Island skipjacks, had been working north earlier in the season in Hooper Straits. The oysters were large there, the catches fair. But as the season wore on the catches declined, prompting today's move, a southerly migration in miniature, reminiscent of the New Englanders' migration and brought on by the same causes.

Four skipjacks, all from Chance, all with their yawl boats hanging in the breeze, sailed in broad meanders on Tangier Sound, among them the *Thomas W. Clyde*. Jack said, "Wherever the *Clyde* stops there's gotta be a few oysters."

"Come on out of there, Butch." Out came Butch from the yawl boat, and aft from the foredeck came the crew to haul her.

"Ought to give us three days power and cut it out the rest of the week," Jack grumbled as the crew hauled. "We're lucky to get the two. If we didn't have them we'd have no boats working." He watched closely as the crew, three to a side along the gunwales, heaved the lines bringing up the yawl boat. "Come on then, not too hard now, you'll break that damn block off her."

The *Helen Virginia* was built in 1948, and rebuilt in varying degrees every year since. This morning it again required repair. In a plywood box just aft of the winders, and driving them, rested the donkey engine. Old, caked with rust and without a muffler, it was salvaged from a

"It cost me a thousand bucks to chop down that tree [to replace the mast]. You make enough to keep going—that's all there is to working the water."

combine. In its rotary configuration, the four-cylinder air-cooled Wisconsin looked ready to propel an airplane, but at the moment it provided no service at all. Jack repeatedly pressed the starter button, eliciting coughs and grinds, but no power.

"What shit's wrong with you this morning?" A belch of black smoke was its only response. Out came the now-dead donkey battery. Off came the fuel-water separator, its clear glass cup containing water sufficient to float an egg, but no fuel. Jackie poured fresh gasoline into the cup, swirled it around and pitched it into Chesapeake Bay.

Jack's grandfather worked the Ella, *the skipjack also once captained by Gary Cooper in the silent epic, "The First Kiss."*

Butch, meanwhile, tightened the port shroud turnbuckle to adjust the tension of the rigging that supported the mast. A ship's mast is held in compression by rigging wires in static tension, a system only as strong as its weakest part, which had failed the previous week. "I had too much canvas up for the shape she's in—right good breeze too." Jack smiled as he said this but grew serious as he looked up at his new blond mast. "It cost me a thousand bucks to chop down that tree. You make enough to keep going—that's all there is to working the water. I put forty-four planks on her this year and twenty-four the last. Also a new centerboard and trunk, deck and cabin, and sails last year. I put eight, nine thousand dollars in her. And I don't believe I'll get it back this year." He paused and lit a Muriel Air Tip. "This is the day you're supposed to stop smoking for a day. Hell, I'd go in if I couldn't smoke. Gets on your nerves, this work."

Like the rigging, Jack's nerves were in dynamic tension, a condition expressed in his day-long shuffle in front of the wheel. In his camouflage jacket, white rubber boots and Sergio Valente corduroys, Jack danced about the aft deck clapping his hands in an effort to quicken the pace of the work, in an effort to keep warm. There was no Captain Bligh in him; he was not larger than life. Of average height and slim build, he was fifty-six and looked forty-five. Were it not for his deeply creased face he'd look comfortably placed clerking the counter at the local hardware store. His authority stemmed from his knowledge of the water and his ownership of the boat. All these Thomases, and Jackie, had crewed for him for years; their reputations were known all around. When something needed doing on the *Helen Virginia*, when the sail needed tending, the donkey engine fueling, the crew would likely see and attend to it unbidden.

Jack's grandfather worked the *Ella*, the skipjack also once captained by Gary Cooper in the silent epic, "The First Kiss." The story of a waterman who forsook oysters for piracy to put his brothers through college, it was filmed in St. Michaels with the entire skipjack fleet serving as extras. "I've still got people up that way," Jack said, "and they's watermen too."

He had often scanned the sky on his way toward the Sound, pausing now and then to look at the sun, which was haloed by a white circle twenty diameters out. Sundog. "Anytime you see a sundog it's gonna rain within twenty-four hour. And the weatherman can't tell you no different. You see it in the evenings most times just before she goes down. It'll rain tonight or tomorrow morning for sure," and with that Jack trained his binoculars on the port of Wenona, on southern Deal Island. "Have nine drudge boats up that way and I don't see none of them coming out. Not yet. Light winds."

⌐∽

Deal Island hangs like a crab claw from a broad marshy neck of mainland Eastern Shore. Just beyond its pincers is Little Deal Island, itself a smaller set of jaws pinching at the broad shallows of Tangier Sound. When Methodism swept like wild fire through the Eastern Shore early in the last century, it spread, more often than not, from the vicinity of Deal Island, in the person of the Rev. Joshua Thomas. Its effects around the Bay have been long lasting, permanently inscribed on roadmaps and navigation charts, as is told in the 1871 biography of Thomas:

> Deal's (or as they were formerly called Devil's) Islands, are two in number, and are situated to the N.E. of Tangier, near the main, and not between the Sound and the Bay. Though the name by which they are now known is a contraction of "Devil's" . . . Rev. D. Dailey while P. E. of the District, used to insist on spelling the name in this way, lest there should seem to be a recognition of Satan's having some right to, or property in them.

Joshua Thomas, who was born and raised a waterman on Tangier Island, had property in them—he owned half of Little Deal Island and used it as the center of his ministry. Setting forth in *The Methodist*, a large, two-sail log canoe, he plied Tangier Sound in search of lost souls, in search of customers for his vegetables and clams. He is perhaps best remembered for exhorting the British, who in 1813 were encamped on Tangier Island, to quit their war-making. Their continued hostilities, he warned, were foreordained by God to failure. The Brits listened, perhaps chuckled, and then sailed for Baltimore and an encounter witnessed by Francis Scott Key. Of Deal and Little Deal islands, Thomas's biographer wrote:

> The larger one (on which there is a good sized Methodist Church, and where camp meetings have been held most of the years since 1828) is about three miles in length, by one in width. It is a very productive soil, suitable for almost any species of grain, fruit, or vegetables. An immense quantity of sweet potatoes is raised here, as also a large yield of corn, and some excellent wheat.

> But the population (numbering nearly one thousand) like that on the smaller islands, has to depend more on the water than on the land for support.

"Good drudging day—I wouldn't want no better. Too much wind and your dredges go too fast."

Deal Island now has about three thousand residents, few fields in production and a continuing dependence on the water. Jack Parkinson was born into a family of skipjack captains and watermen and raised in Wenona, never leaving until called to serve in Korea. When he returned he married and moved to Chance, on the mainland side of Upper Thorofare, the harbor separating Deal Island from the Eastern Shore mainland.

"All right, get her up. Shake that reef out of her." Up went the mainsail, her hoops binding on the swelling mast as the sail tugged them. Steve and Butch crawled along the bowsprit and set the jib. The *Helen Virginia*, under full canvas, was ready to catch oysters.

"Oyster rocks right here, and all the way south, nothing but oyster rocks," Jack said as he surveyed calm waters, giving depth to their flat surface.

"Rest of them boats been getting twenty-five to thirty as I been catching ten to twelve. Was time to come on down here. First time I be down here this year. You never know. We'll see how she goes."

A light northeasterly breeze luffed the foresail, which then billowed and filled. The *Helen Virginia*, out for oysters, heeled and surged.

"Go wind'ard."

The windward dredge emerged full with oysters. "Look at all these little ones. Tons of them. As many as you want of them. Whole dredges of them. They never do grow here though. Don't nobody know why."

The bar reached, the work having started, the tenor of the day now varied with the size of the catch and the strength of the wind. The crew carried on instructed only by the incessant throttling of the donkey engine, whose exhaust mingled with cigarette and cigar smoke, and with comments that hung in the breeze.

"Wind's picking up. Could be east but I can't see no land. Probably northeast."

"Good drudging day—I wouldn't want it no better. Too much wind and your dredges go too fast. I'd had about three bushels if I went to the Straits today. You need a lot of wind on that hard bottom."

"Put a reef in her. Take a little centerboard in."

"I don't know where in the hell those other boats have been—looks like they haven't come out."

Again came the dredges, full and fast. Lower them away, and again the crew dropped to their knees. Bending over the sprawling spill from the dredges, they appeared canine as they tossed oysters back between their legs onto the mounds.

"Go."

"Lot of small oysters down this way. Lot of them. Get the same price—though they're harder to cull. The ones up the Straits worth three dollar more a bushel—they're fatter, yield more to the bushel, but we're getting the same price. That's just the way it is. That's all. Ain't no sense in any of it."

"You get more on power days because you can go round in circles over those little hills, see. It's not that you're faster, you just maneuver better. A place like this you can catch as many with sails as you can with power—the oysters all spread out, not in those hills."

"Keep your men picking in the oysters—that's the only sure thing to drudging. If they get you a few everytime you'll have some."

"Number was one-thirteen last night. I had a triple-one and a one-sixteen." Maryland State Lottery Pick Three.

"Damn. They're all in port, everyone a them. You take a chance coming out on a day like today, wind like it is."

"Wind's dying now. Weren't for this wind dying we would have had forty to fifty today by sail. May yet."

"Sundog's back. Lookie here. Sure sign."

"You don't need much wind with all this stuff on the bottom. All you need to do is pull them about half the length of this boat."

"Look at all those dead oysters in there. Ain't nobody knows the reason for it. Ain't no pollution killed them, cause there ain't no pollution down this way."

"Catch is half, but price double last year's. Don't nobody know why. It'll come out about even but you put more time in it. It's an all-day job now."

"You make enough to survive, that's all there is to working the water. Except you go where you want and when you want. That's the best part of it."

The wind dropped, the foresail luffed, flapped in the erratic breeze, then hung. The *Helen Virginia*, her windward dredge in the water, stalled.

"Damn."

"You never know what you'll do, what'll happen. You take chance with you every morning."

THE PRIVILEGE OF THE WATER

Hampton Roads, Late March, 6:30 A.M.

I t's a cat's cradle of intersecting courses and cross purposes. Aircraft carriers this way, oil barges that, the odd hydroplane speeding off somewhere else. And through it all, thirty feet below, blue crabs are settled in the cold mud, their metabolism on low, awaiting the arrival of spring. For Cap'n Willy Forrest this was a day like thousands that had come before, and yet it was also like none other. This was a day Willy Forrest would spend dredging hard crabs, and it would be his last.

He had left the Graham and Rollins Seafood dock in Hampton at 6:30 A.M., piloting the *Louisa Bush* through Hampton Roads, past large freighters slack on their moorings, and out to the mouth of the Chesapeake Bay.

~

Wintertime dredging is for the crabs that got away. As the Chesapeake's waters cooled with the arrival of autumn, the crabs not caught by Wadey Murphy, Danny Beck, Morris Marsh and their brethren settled down into the mud for the winter. The males settled into the nearest deep channel. Many of the females made a journey of up to two hundred miles to the mouth of the Bay, to the southern capes, where they, too, burrowed in the mud to await spring. Like oysters, clams and fish, crabs can't regulate their body temperature. Whatever the prevailing water temperature, within a few degrees the crab's internal temperature is the same, and as its temperature drops, so, too, does its rate of metabolism. Burrowed for the winter, it doesn't feed or move; it lies still, in a kind of suspended animation. Because overwintering crabs won't come to the bait, the wintertime crabber's work is much like the oysterman's—he dredges the floor of the Bay. Dragging a device much like a large oyster dredge, the Chesapeake's crab dredgers crisscross the Bay's mouth, describing courses governed by concentrations of female blue crabs.

Cap'n Willy was one of only two on that early March morning to be dredging in the traditional way, from large decked-over vessels with dredges pulled from each side. The boats were of a model once used as buy boats on the Chesapeake—boats that would come to oyster bars and buy oysters from the watermen working there—or as freighters. Modeled after sailing bugeyes, they were high-sided and stoutly built, and as much as fifty feet on deck. There's not much use for such a boat on the Chesapeake anymore. Freight doesn't move on the water in such small quantities, and oystermen now take their catches back to the dock. To maintain a large vessel solely for wintertime dredging is not economical, and Chesapeake crab dredgers now work from open workboats that pull a single dredge from the stern, boats that can be profitably used for crab potting in the summer. And so, for the *Louisa Bush* and the *Catherine*, both owned by Graham and Rollins Seafood in Hampton, this would be their last season dredging hard crabs.

There was nothing mournful in this passing to Cap'n Willy. He lived on the Back River, just north of Hampton, thirty miles south of Mobjack Bay, a block up from where his father was born and raised. Under Virginia's more liberal leasing laws, he held two hundred acres of leased oyster bottom. And when he looked out from his yard, he looked out on the waters of the Back River. If he was of a mind to, he could go any day to his oyster bottom and pull a few licks. The passing of his days as a crab dredger would not take him from the water, and he would not miss them. If it didn't make sense to work the larger boats, let the smaller ones come on. Graham and Rollins would have the *Louisa Bush* work as long as Cap'n Willy agreed to work her, and for

The passing of his days as a crab dredger would not take him from the water and he would not miss them.

Cap'n Willy the time had come to work her no longer.

Lofty cirrus clouds highlighted a bright warm morning. The seas were calm. The *Louisa Bush* plodded along the edge of the Hampton Roads shipping channel toward Thimble Shoals, four miles west of the mouth of the Bay. Lying about the aft cabin, lulled to sleep by the throb of the diesel were Kenny and David, the day's crew, transients, fishermen till the next check, local Hampton youths, neither long out of high school. David had crewed "drudge boats," as they are sometimes called, but for Kenny this day would be his whole career, his apprenticeship, journeywork and retirement all in one day. In the pilot house, Cap'n Willy stood behind a large spoked wooden wheel and tracked a familiar course.

Willy's family had sailed the Chesapeake as long as he could remember. His father had tonged oysters, had run freight—oyster seed by the bushel, watermelons by the ton—and had apprenticed his son as soon as Willy could walk. Every holiday, any day he had off from school, Willy would accompany his father, first to cull oysters, later to tong. And at an early age he quit school to follow the water full time. "I met my daddy at the landing one day and I told him, I said, 'The school gives me the headache. I ain't going to school no more.' Well, he tried to talk me into going to school. I should of went, but I was just as big a guy as he was when I was fourteen years old. He wasn't very big and he couldn't talk me into going back. So he put me on the boat. He carried me up the James River and we stayed on the boat a whole week. He tried to work my daggone hide off—thought I'd go back to school the next year. As the next year got ready, he said, 'Well, you're going to school, aren't you?' I said, 'Yeah, I'm going to *your* school.' Me and him, we worked together from then on."

At 8:00 Cap'n Willy slowed the diesel, signaling David and Kenny forward to the deck. Each to a side, they heaved the starboard dredge over the roller, its chain chattering through a pulley mounted atop what looked like the six-foot stub of a former mast, and through a five-inch deckpipe to the winch below. When the chain had payed out, a large steel hook was slipped under a link to take pressure off the winch. Each to a side, they heaved the port dredge. Cap'n

Willy throttled up the diesel. The *Louisa Bush* began to dredge.

"I'm looking for a hot goose today," Cap'n Willy said. "You see we call a good spot a hot goose. If there ain't many crabs, we say the feathers's been picked off." He giggled and raised an arm as if to elbow an old buddy. "Of course, there ain't many feathers left," he went on. "One lick and you'll have fifty crabs and the next you'll have twenty. This late and the crabs start moving around. Can't catch them with the dredge if they ain't buried. This time of year it's just something to do in the wintertime, this is. I wasn't going to do this no more, but they talked me into one more year. Today will wind it up for me."

When his youngest brother finished school, Willy took him working as a tonger. According to their secret plan, the two would make enough money to pay their ailing father to stay home, but their father wouldn't hear of it. "My daddy said, 'No sir, as long as I'm able to get these legs to move me up on that boat, y'all ain't going to pay *me* to stay home. I'm going with y'all.' " Willy's father lived till his seventy-sixth year, and had asthma all his life. But in his day, Willy said, he could tong more oysters than anyone.

Cap'n Willy motored the *Louisa Bush* into the sun for ten minutes. Held steady in the freshening westerly breeze and steepening swells, she rode low from the drag of the dredges, straining against reins of chain. Cap'n Willy pulled a thin steel wire on the port side of the pilot house. The port chain slackened, the hook dropped, the dredge came slowly up from the bottom. When it reached the gunwale roller David and Kenny grabbed its rings and spilled its contents onto the deck. Three whelk, one railroad spike, several large stones, two pieces of coal, a dozen oyster shells, a couple of bushels of rope grass and ten crabs, two of them dead. They threw the live crabs into large barrels and shoveled the rest over the side. "I used to keep that coal and burn it in my fireplace at home," Cap'n Willy said. "There's plenty of it down there—coalers used to run through here all the time. There's plenty of everything down there but crabs." He lit his pipe and then pulled a thin steel wire on the starboard side. The starboard dredge came up holding five crabs—two horseshoe, three spider, none blue. Cap'n Willy grimaced at the contents of the dredges. "This is a really boring job this time of year," he said. The crew swung the dredges back over the rollers.

On every horizon, as the *Louisa Bush* ranged over Thimble Shoals dragging her dredges, were ships of a number and variety found nowhere else on the Bay. There were freighters, and yachts—the Intracoastal Waterway wends past Thimble Shoals on its way to Norfolk and points south. Mostly there were naval vessels—Newport News shipyard and Norfolk, site of the largest naval installation on the Atlantic Coast, were just up the channel through Hampton Roads. A large flock of surf scoters off to starboard floated in the path of a black missile sub that pushed before it a churning white-and-gray mound. "They's coming through here all the time," Cap'n Willy said. He pointed westward, toward looming silhouettes moving slowly in tandem. "Now them there's airplane carriers, and over there, that's a frigate. We see a lot of them, what with the Navy down here."

After a stint in the Navy during the Second World War, Willy returned to find that his father had amassed enough lumber to build a dredge boat. And by the winter of 1947, father and son had her ready to dredge crabs. They'd go out with two dredges and catch, in those days before harvest limits, as many as eighty barrels a day, as many as three barrels in a single lick. In the fall they'd used her to run seed oysters to Lynnhaven and to Back River, getting paid by freight, so much on the bushel. Three, four months of the year freighting oysters, the winter dredging crabs. And during the summer they'd take a smaller boat to tong oysters from their own leased bed. Crabbing in winter, oystering in summer, freighting in autumn.

Fifteen minutes into another lick of the Bay floor the starboard dredge came up with an assortment of life not found elsewhere in the Chesapeake. Blackcheek tonguefish, mantis shrimp, smelt, oyster toadfish, ponderous arks, and whelks. Coal, ballast stones, and fossil scallop shells. And some few blue crabs. David tossed seven blue crabs into the barrel. Kenny, a slender black man of muscular build, had never before set foot on a boat, had never seen sea life. Anything coming up in the dredge that he couldn't identify, everything but blue crabs, he picked out from the dredge spoil, and held up to the light. Whatever it was, he pulled at it and poked it and slid it along the deck. Then he placed it in a galvanized bucket brimming with water—thought he might start an aquarium. Cap'n Willy looked down on all this from the open wheelhouse windows and giggled. "That fella's hell on seafood, isn't he?"

When the freighting played out, Willy and his father kept the boat up for dredging crabs, but a time came when the price plunged for two seasons running, plunged so low they could barely cover expenses. "I decided to get rid of it, and I got so fed up with it I practically give the boat away," said Willy. "I tried crab potting once. I made a hundred of them when they first came on and fished them twice. The price dropped a dollar each time. Then I put them on the dump. And I said to my buddy, 'When they jump you take them.' He took four or five a day until they were gone. You'd do alright potting in the spring when the price was high, but the minute they could, the buyers would cut the price on you. You couldn't make a living on that. You'd pay the price when you'd go to buy crab meat—they never cut that price—but they'd cut the price when you went and caught the crabs."

Horsehoe crabs, blood arks, and bushel on bushel of rope grass, up in the dredges. "Just look at all that rope grass," Cap'n Willy said. "It strikes when the water gets cold. Gets so thick the dredges float right over it." (Rope grass is not a grass at all, really, but a hydroid, a distant relative to sea nettles, a carnivore that paralyzes its hapless victims.)

Willy then returned to dredging, captaining other dredge boats, working by percentage. He worked four or five different boats out of Hampton, until the city began the restoration of its harbor. The waterfront development plan didn't include much space for watermen, and the business Willy worked for had to sell out, leaving him without a boat to work. Eventually, he found another, worked her for a few years, and then came to Graham and Rollins. He had been working there for the last six or seven years. When Willy began working at Graham and Rollins the company had twelve boats dredging crabs. By this year the fleet had diminished to two, the *Catherine* and the *Louisa Bush*.

Three spotted hake, two menhaden, a six-inch pipe fish, a twelve-inch flounder, a second

"I went to Oklahoma once with the wife. Supposed to stay two weeks. I didn't last but six days. I get sick when I'm away from the water."

bucket pressed into service. LCI's, landing craft island, LCD's, landing craft dock, navy gray, twenty-five knots.

Willy figured he had done all right, thought he had made the right choice when he chose to follow the water. "I got two brothers that work the shipyards. And they don't like the shipyards—they like the water too. But they was always afraid they's going to starve. They thought they could do better in the shipyard. And so they goes to work there every day and dreads going there. I've always enjoyed what I do. My daddy told me, 'Don't matter what you do, you be happy what you're doing.' So I took his advice and that's why I've ended up on the water. I guess you could say I was driven to it. If you don't got no drive to work the water, then you just don't get it. I went to Oklahoma once with the wife. Supposed to stay two weeks. I didn't last but six days. I get sick when I'm away from the water."

Frigate ship, hydroplane, coal freighter. The starboard dredge held seven crabs. Listless and slow when they emerged from the water, the crabs worked up a passable scamper after a few minutes in the full sun. "Yesterday at 12:30 we had a barrel and a half." Cap'n Willy said. "It gets worse every day." Now, at 11:15, on the deck of the *Louisa Bush* was less than one barrel of crabs.

"My son done got his masters now. And he went to school this summer to get his captain's license. My grandson likes the water too,

likes it just as good as I do. My son, I forced his education on him. He didn't want to go, but I was bigger than he was. If my daddy would of treat me like that, I guess I'd a got an education too. I got my son about twenty acres of oyster bottom and in the summertime he works that. I have two hundred acres oyster bottom, and if the water weren't so polluted I could live off that all year. That's what's got everybody. That and MSX. It hit here about twenty-seven years ago. We had two of the biggest oyster packers in the world and they's gone now. They'd plant seed oysters out in the Bay—they'd plant millions of seed—but it got so as soon as they'd put them out they'd die, wouldn't live a year. They'd plant them where we dredge crabs, but you won't see any oysters out there now."

By 3:30 there were three barrels of crabs on the forward deck. The wind had picked up to fifteen knots, westerly, the rollers to three feet. The last haul of the dredge on the starboard side held a fourteen-inch flounder, which Kenny rolled like a parchment and squeezed into the bucket. "When you see those, spring is right around the corner," Cap'n Willy said. Cap'n Willy had his own collection of sea life—a large net spans his living room wall. From its webbing hang oyster shells, starfish, bottles, spear heads, German silver, items he's dredged from the mouth of the Bay. Every so often, as Kenny had grabbed at some artifact of the deep, Cap'n Willy would throw open the pilot house window and shout, "Hey, I got one of those in my net." Now, as he pulled the winch wire for the last time, Cap'n Willy said, "I'd like to have dredged me a chest of gold."

"I'd like to have dredged me a chest of gold."

Cap'n Willy headed back at 4:00. His catch of three-and-a-half barrels was washed, steamed, then spilled on stainless steel tables where eighteen women would pick them. Cap'n Willy didn't linger long at the dock on his last day dredging crabs. He stood around a few minutes as the crabs were lowered into a hopper for washing and then went on home.

"I decided I was getting too old for drudging, so I quit. We had problems getting a crew. You'd have to pick them off the street, you couldn't get nobody experienced to go, or to stay once you got them. So I just got fed up with it, and me and the other boy from the *Catherine* told the fella there at Graham and Rollins the best thing to do was get rid of them boats and buy crabs. And now he's getting all the crabs he want—gets them out of Tangier, gets them out of Carolina, gets crabs everywhere."

After a lifetime on the water, Willy Forrest would now settle into retirement. From his living room he would look out over the Back River, and, when he's of a mind to, he would go to his leased bed and pull a few licks. He'd stay close to the water.

"About eight or nine years ago a couple came here from Old Dominion College and they wanted to know if I was interested in cleaning up the Bay. So I joined up with that Bay Foundation. I gave those folks ten bucks, and I told them if it did any good to come back and get more. They told me not to expect no miracles, that it'd take years to clean it up. I know they're working on it. And I believe there's been progress. It just takes time."

"Yeah," he said, "I'd like to see my grandchildren have the same privilege of the water as I've had."

OVER THE LINE

Cox Creek, The End of March, 8:30 A.M.

"If we see the man coming you're going to have to get in the water right quick—we don't want to mess this up again. This is our last chance."

These were the final instructions of George O'Donnell, captain of the workboat *Night Moves*, to Jay Snyder, commercial oyster diver, just before Jay jumped into the thick gray waters of Cox Creek. Jay stood close and listened attentively. Then he nodded, spat into his mask, climbed onto the washboard, and disappeared over the side.

Title 02, chapter 4, section 9, paragraph H, of the Maryland Department of Natural Resources Laws and Regulations Concerning the Commercial Harvest of Oysters, Clams, Conchs, Surf Clams and Ocean Quahogs says that "Oysters may be taken only by hand tongs in . . . all the waters northerly of a line drawn from the Southwestern tip of Turkey Point to Cox Creek Light 2 to Cox Creek Daybeacon 1 then continuing to shore."

George, who was Secretary and Treasurer of the Maryland Commercial Oyster Divers Association, had no trouble reading. Nor was he unfamiliar with local waters. O'Donnells four generations back have rounded Turkey Point, have worked Cox Creek. But George was not simply pushing the line—he was well over it and closing in on an oyster bar reserved for harvest only by hand tong.

George was also pushing a point. "That line," he said, "represents discrimination, pure and simple." And thus his hope that when he contested the ticket he felt sure he would get from the Maryland Marine Police that morning, he would win a fairer deal for himself and his fellow divers from the courts. And it would be a fairer deal, he thought, than he had gotten from the Maryland General Assembly and the Department of Natural Resources, which George sees as favoring hand tongers.

Who, after all, would want to dive cold murky waters foraging for oysters?

It also wouldn't bother him if he caught a few oysters in the meanwhile.

Until 1973, it had been the law in Maryland that divers could harvest only one bushel of oysters a day, and only for personal consumption. It was called "sport diving" in the book of regulations, and further regulation seemed unnecessary—who, after all, would want to dive cold murky waters foraging for oysters? Brett Thom, a sport diver out of Annapolis, was one of a few who did. In 1972 he arranged to be ticketed for catching slightly more than one bushel of oysters. He took his ticket to court and won.

The following season found several divers working as oystermen for the first time. Among them was Ray Mathieson, a commercial and recreational diver, a salvage and rescue diver, a person with facility around abandoned offshore underwater freighters but a newcomer to oystering. Ray had his winters free, mostly, and in his recumbent, relaxing hours he imagined money scattered about in hummocky mounds swelling from the Chesapeake's bottom, flattened pyramids of calcitic gold waiting to be plucked from the Bay floor. Of course, there would be a few techniques to master along the way.

Without the decades of trial and error that preceded other Chesapeake oyster fisheries, and with the same daily need to survive in the marketplace, a few techniques would prove a lot to learn quickly. How should oysters be transported to the surface? In baskets how large, how tethered, how made? How can the diver signal the tender that one basket is filled and that another is needed? Should the diver carry his air strapped to his back in SCUBA tanks, or breathe it from an onboard compressor? The answers to these questions would prove up the claim on Ray's imagination.

Diving from a sixty- by twenty-foot clamming scow that first season, Ray tested the suitability of SCUBA gear and the reliability of automatic retrieval devices that would haul huge crates of oysters from the Bay floor, crates so large they also served to anchor the scow in the Chesapeake's wintertime northerly gales. The scow was not like the usual workboat, more a river barge superstructured with a greenhouse. With sail area the size of a bungalow, the scow needed a lot of anchor. But whatever the weather outside, the climate inside was warm and moist, almost tropical. And Ray could step from this Aruba or St. Thomas right into the Chesapeake, through a trough cut into the scow's flat bottom. But it was too slow, this floating box, making only three knots, a figure that would dip to zero before dropping into negative numbers when bucking a head wind.

For the second season Ray brought down from New Jersey a retired marine police boat. While not a traditional workboat, it would at least better approximate one with its small cabin and large cockpit. SCUBA was given over to a surface compressor, the large ungainly crates to smaller rectangular wire baskets with wooden lids that would automatically close when hauled from the Bay floor. Gradually Ray further refined techniques and gear, and in these refinements an adaptation to local conditions would refine his thinking. Dive boats would come to resemble workboats, would at last become workboats, for the same reason workboats are commonly used —they have little windage, these low-slung, small-cabined craft; one can hold his place on the bar.

At first divers worked deeper bars which the hand tongers could not, or cared not to. The divers worked the Wye River and the Chester. They worked Eastern Bay. They worked pockets of Eastern Shore water near the eastern terminus of the Bay Bridge, to shorten their commute from the western shore.

Hand tongers paid little notice to the fledgling efforts, all of it derisive. But then, a few hand tongers, those whose catches weren't all they'd hoped, those whose own brief attempts at diving hadn't succeeded, began to grumble. Who were these western shore sportsmen come to pick our beds clean? Isolated grumblings finally prompted the divers to form the Maryland Commercial Divers Association in response.

Then there came the massive deep-water oyster die-offs. First in 1978, then again in 1982, and 1984 and then continuously, the Chesapeake's depths no longer supported oysters. Not merely did they not support them, they seemed to wipe them out wholesale. Foreshadowing these deep-water deaths were MSX and Dermo, two diseases that first visited the Chesapeake during the late 1950s and now reappeared whenever summertime droughts moved saline waters far up the Bay. The oystermen knew MSX and Dermo, in pattern if not in name—if the weather is dry, the water is salty, the oysters die—a combined threat that was imprinted into their expectations much like the weather itself. What they hadn't expected, much less understood, was anoxia, the Chesapeake's deep-water killer.

Nutrients, nitrogen and phosphorus, from farm fields and from sewage treatment plants, from recreational boats, from golf courses and backyard lawns, nitrogen by the ton from acid rain, flowed into the estuary at ever-increasing rates and in volumes greater than the Chesapeake could healthfully accommodate. And here another line was crossed, a line that had nothing to do with fishing rights or depth of good water but that would ultimately influence both—an invisible line measured in abstract ecological terms such as "carrying capacity of the environment," a line separating nutrient sufficiency from glut.

For longer and longer periods the Chesapeake's deep waters grew lethal. Winds, strong easterlies, or westerlies, sloshed dead water over the oyster beds. And, where it remained long enough, it killed the disease-weakened oysters. The divers decompressed and swam into the shallows.

Already working in the shallows, rigidly riding a tradition that gave them exclusive use of the tributaries, were hand tongers. The divers weren't working fair, they grumbled, they're picking out the best and leaving us the dregs. The grousing again grew louder, capturing this

For longer and longer periods the Chesapeake's deep waters grew lethal. Winds...sloshed dead water over the oyster beds. And where it remained long enough, it killed disease-weakened oysters.

time the ears of sympathetic Eastern Shore legislators, some of whom set about restricting the divers, none of whom then thought to trace the reason or remedy for the deep-water carnage. Led by Eastern Shore legislators, in 1983 the Maryland General Assembly passed a law that set the dived-oyster cull size, the smallest oyster a diver may harvest, to four inches, one full inch above the standard applied to other oyster harvesters. They reduced the daily catch limit for dive boats to thirty bushels (the hand tongers got twenty-five bushels per man to a maximum of seventy-five per boat, dredge boats got one hundred and fifty), and the areas available to oyster divers they restricted dramatically.

"When that four-inch cull law was proposed we laughed and knew it was unconstitutional," George said. "We thought it'd never go through—now I think anything would make it through that legislature."

The difference between three- and four-inch oysters, given the current condition of the Chesapeake's oyster beds, was the difference between scratching out a living and going broke. Those watermen who continued diving—half gave it up and returned to the tong, or to wintertime desks and summertime salvage diving—violated the law en masse. They'd get what legal oysters they could and then hide the rest. They'd hide them in boat cabins, or in the beds of pickup trucks. They'd submerge them in the shallows. Then they'd go back at night to retrieve them. Like fences and thieves, packers and watermen would meet on lonely back roads in the early morning hours and then part, one truck made lighter, one made heavier, and no one made the wiser.

"It climaxed six weeks before the law was thrown out," George said. "Different tongers would see us hiding oysters and turn us in. The Marine Police handled it very well until they got too many complaints. As it was, a lot of them thanked us after it was all over because it saved them a lot of hassle—phone calls in the middle of the night to catch packers that had gone down the road to secretly buy oysters, or watermen who were sinking their bushels and bringing them back up." Before it was all over, eight divers with "inadvertent citations," a phrase George used to describe infractions not intentionally sought to test the law, went to court. Judge Clark, of the Queen Anne's district, threw the cull size provision of the law out as unconstitutional. Discrimination, pure and simple. Soon other district judges in other Maryland counties made similar rulings; they threw out the discriminatory cull-size provision. The following year the General Assembly would follow suit.

The two other provisions of the original law remained. Most divers could tolerate the lower boat limit—nobody catches the limit after the first few weeks of the season anyway. What they couldn't live with, what was especially irksome in a time of deep-water die-offs, were the limits on harvest area, those imaginary lines marking oyster bars they weren't allowed to work. Hand tongers, many divers believed, began the season in unrestricted waters where divers worked, transitional waters neither shallow nor deep. And after raking those beds clean, they retreated to the shallows, to beds that had hitherto gone unharvested and where the divers weren't allowed. That the divers couldn't abide. Against that they would go over the line.

What they couldn't live with, what was especially irksome in a time of deep-water die-offs, were the limits on harvest area. That the divers couldn't abide.

~

It began at 6:30 on the morning of this, the next-to-last day of the oyster season, the next-to-last day of March. Bennett Point landing, Wye River. George pulled his GMC pickup to the bulkhead and hopped down into a green punt to paddle out to his workboat, *Night Moves*.

Bennett Point landing fronts a small cove of the Wye River bordered by ornamental maples and oaks and a stately mansard-roofed house whose luxuriant lawn carpets the river's edge. Unlike rivers of the lower Eastern Shore, unlike the Nanticoke a day's sail south, the Wye is intimate, close in. Its banks are densely canopied with sycamore and oak, maple and pine, understoried with holly, laurel and dogwood, overrun with deer. (Overrun, too, with wealth, old Eastern Shore wealth of the kind brought down by Rockefellers and DuPonts during the last century, new unsettled wealth, fresh across the Bay Bridge from suburban Washington and Baltimore and Annapolis.) Bennett Point itself is now graced with a lighthouse, but not one placed there for purposes of navigation. "That's when you know you've made it," George said, "when you have your own lighthouse."

In the summertime, the Wye River is also overrun with sportsmen, more so than any other Eastern Shore river. They come by the hundreds in the early morning to trotline for crabs, to fish and to sail. They came in such numbers to the Bennett Point boat ramp that watermen would return at day's end with full crab baskets only to carry them for blocks past parked cars and trailers to load their trucks. Watermen complained to the county. Could the ramp be removed? We can't appropriate money for alterations, the county responded, only for repairs. Does the existing structure require repair? It soon did—under a cloak of darkness persons unknown tore apart the structure; they tore out the ramp. County workers then came to extend the bulkhead.

Now, mostly watermen use Bennett Point landing. Parked on its adjoining gravel lot on any given morning before dawn are Fords and Chevys, GMCs and Dodges, pickups all, full size, American made, their beds loaded with baskets, or buoys, or line. "QUIT BEEFING, EAT SEAFOOD," their bumpers implore. And just beyond, gently pulling at stakes driven into the Wye's soft bottom, are workboats, many of them dive boats. George tethered his punt to the stake, and motored Night Moves to the bulkhead to wait for Jay.

Thirty minutes later, Jay rolled up in a narrow Japanese pickup, an Isuzu Pup. "Jay, get that clock from the cabin when you get a chance," George said to him as he hopped on board, a point that hit wide of the mark.

Soon, with a low throb Night Moves made way for the channel, George steering from the cabin, Jay beside him inspecting his gear and munching down a breakfast of peanut butter and jelly sandwiches. The cabin was close and cluttered, its ceiling smudged with soot from a Kero-Sun heater, its windows fogged with smoke and soot and wave wash. The swinging cabin door framed brighter vistas, Eastern Bay red and misty in early morning, warm in early spring.

Jay began to put on his gear. Wool socks over wool socks, sweat pants over Durafold long underwear, under Patagonia capilene polyester. Over all, a dry suit with integral boots and hood and a pressure relief valve on the upper arm. Then weights, thirty-two pounds of rectangular lead threaded onto a woven nylon belt, flippers, backpack, regulator, gloves. The gloves were preheated with water drawn from a bucket that would remain perched daylong on the Kero-Sun heater. Finally, just before he went over the side, Jay donned his mask, with its integral regulator, and held on tight.

Now Jay Snyder was picking over the bottom of Cox Creek, while George O'Donnell stood topside culling oysters, keeping watch. 8:30 A.M. George had arranged for someone to report his infraction at 9:00. In the meantime the oysters came up in fair numbers.

Jay circled out from *Night Moves*, his position evident from the meandering trail of bubbles floating up from his regulator. As with most commercial divers, Jay used a compressor, a small, two-cylinder rig powered by a Briggs & Stratton I/C Industrial Commercial Cast Iron Bore air-cooled motor. Crimped onto its intake tubes were two long plastic pipes that flailed about like antennae. They went skyward, above the cabin top, protecting the air intake from the compressor's exhaust. The compressor pumped air into a pressure tank, to which was attached a bright yellow air line also tethered to Jay's back. (During the colder months, when subsurface waters may go subfreezing, divers spike their pressure tanks with grain alcohol or some preferred spirit to prevent regulator freeze-up.)

The catch was fair, the weather bright—the anticipated rain hadn't materialized—the season about over.

It had been alleged that diving was too efficient, that divers would pick the beds clean. To counter this point George had statistics "from the DNR themselves" that showed diving as the least efficient of oyster harvesting methods as measured in catch per man hour. Interpreting these statistics, lending an air of scientific respectability to the diver's position, was Robert W. Brody of Marine Ecology and Fisheries Biology, Inc., a biologist the association hired to analyze and respond to the Department of Natural Resources' restrictions on cull size and harvest areas, and whose report George had also brought with him. When he got the chance George would speak with the austere certainty of science, naked and objective, when he spoke for diving.

"Every gear has certain advantages or no one would use that gear," he said. "When the oysters are thick the tongers have an advantage, they'll catch more than we will. When they're thin we do better."

"We harvest premium-quality oysters. It's like picking apples—they're hand picked and we don't disturb the bed."

George continued in this vein, while waiting for his encounter with the marine police, conveying the way he saw it from the cockpit of his boat. And not only could one feel the fervor in his position, one could also see his point. No western shore newcomer arriving to pick the beds clean, George is Eastern Shore born and raised. He had hand tonged himself, and would work now alongside the hand tongers he had known his life long, in waters he had worked most of his thirty years, that his family had worked for four generations, were it not for his vision of faceless persons at the Maryland General Assembly and the Department of Natural Resources, who, while sitting at desks far removed from the water, drew imaginary lines and moved them up the tributaries, causing George's income to move down in proportion.

George culled out a basket and, with a sweep of his hand, pushed the spat-laden shells overboard. "We put back an oyster for every one we take. This proves the Bay will produce life, whether it will sustain it is the overriding question." George O'Donnell would run, next season, for the office of President of the Maryland Commercial Divers' Association.

Jay surfaced and climbed the black metal ladder at the back of the boat. He reached for his water bottle. The air he breathed was dry, the compressor also a condenser, squeezing the water vapor in the pressure tank until it coalesced into droplets that collected in the bottom, leaving behind air that might have blown off the Sahara directly into Jay's throat. Every hour or so he ascended to the oasis.

"Not too bad through here, is it?"

"No, not too bad. Muddy though."

It had been alleged that diving was too efficient, that divers would pick the beds clean.

Jay Snyder, underwaterman, waxed philosophical on oyster diving: "It's as much cerebral as physical exercise," he said, "just like running. It's time to yourself to think about things. But you have to be comfortable. If you get in the water and everything is just right—no water coming into your suit, gloves in good shape—you're going to have a pretty good day. If there's any discomfort, the day is bad. When you're oyster diving it's not like a real job. I've busted my ass for forty bucks a night tending bar in less than ideal working conditions. That puts a whole new perspective on work. Oyster diving's not all that bad." Pausing to reflect on the enormity of his admission, his brow a deep furrow of reservation, he added, "It's a crazy business, though. I don't think five years down the road you'll see me oyster diving."

As he worked, George's eyes roamed over Eastern Bay, focusing now back toward the Wye. "When the law comes, they'll be coming around Bodkin Island, around Turkey Point."

He separated a two-inch oyster from his cull and held it up like a baby at an oyster roast. "The Bay is producing enough life, it's just not sustaining it," he said.

"That call is made by now—we'll see them sometime in the next hour, 9:30 to 10:00, probably."

By 10:15 George was borderline edgy, tending toward piously indignant. George O'Donnell on the marine police: "Anytime you want the son of a bitch you can't find him. In Talbot County they're cruising around all the time. Here in Queen Anne's we have an on-call police force."

Jay was up again. The tide was slackening, its current no longer carrying away the sediment he stirred from the bottom. He motioned for a change of venue, and took a drink of water.

"All right," George replied. "Was it better where we started at?"

"You got to constantly move when the tide stops, otherwise you get a mud-puddle effect," Jay explained as he climbed onto the washboard, and then added, just before the splash, "It's like a small atomic bomb going off."

"If you get in the water and everything is just right—no water coming into your suit, gloves in good shape—you're going to have a pretty good day."

At 11:15, there, rounding Bodkin Island, a cabin cruiser. "That may be the man," George said, but the man passed, the police cruiser *West River* steaming north at full bore. Jay apparently heard the engines or propellers; he surfaced immediately and looked north. He paused, wading momentarily, and then dove back to the rock below.

"They'd rather not do this either," George muttered impatiently. "They're just typical state employees interested in not rocking the boat."

The *West River* drifted, inexplicably, well north in the upper reaches of Cox Creek. Time stood still. George culled diligently, his eyes fixed in focus on the culling board. Without a sideways glance, he artfully spilled oysters from a nearly full basket into an empty of equal size, which then looked generously rounded.

"Are they heading this way?"

The *West River* again climbed to a plane, steaming south. It throttled back abruptly as it passed and then drifted fifty yards aport, giving Jay time to clear the water.

"You're in the hand tonging area."

"Well, do what you got to do. I have no problem with you."

"I'm not going to write any tickets. Tomorrow's my last day. Other folks can write the ticket."

Officer Burnhardt had served in the Maryland Marine Police for thirty years, would retire tomorrow, and would rather not return to court as the issuing officer in a legal maneuver that could take months. Other folks could write the ticket.

George boarded the *West River* as Jay stood in the cockpit in respectful silence. He stood apart but not above these proceedings, a commercial diver working as a waterman, feeling like a diver. "I'm not a waterman," he said. "George is a waterman. I consider myself more an opportunist. If I had several lives to live I might spend one doing this. I just answered an ad in the paper. If they outlawed diving I doubt seriously that I'd tong. Another year doing this, maybe."

George hopped back aboard. The expression on his face was not so much convicted felon as caught schoolboy. "We got to dump three bushels—they'll give us a confiscation receipt later."

As the *West River* hovered a few yards aport, George grabbed three bushels of hand-picked, culled oysters and dumped them over the side—almost into the laps of two hand tongers. "I bet they appreciate that," George said. "OK, let's get the hell out of here."

"So the Association owes us sixty dollars for three bushels," he said as he turned *Night Moves* south.

Jay stared, transfixed, at the sight of the dumping. "Boy, I bet that's a pretty sight down there—those three bushels."

George, or at least part of him, was still aboard the *West River*, reliving moments of high drama. "Hey, he's an officer and a gentleman—no shit, no fuss, just professionally doing his job. And the son of a bitch is like a fox. He don't ask no questions. He knows what's going on."

"Yeah, he's a good man," Jay affirmed vacantly, still looking back to where the oysters were dumped. "Boy, you look at an oyster and it's such a timid thing. So much fuss around it."

"Well, we got the job done," George said in consoling summation.

"Boy, if they do change the lines, I'd like to come back next year. But it's all relative—we'd catch more and get less."

George and Jay went back over the line, back around Turkey Point to the Wye River to work for a while, but the day ended early with a smaller than usual catch.

"We could've caught more, but it was a screwed-up day, really," George said as he stuffed the crates with their lines. "The three bushels was the small part of it as I see it—that ticket could be worth three hundred thousand dollars based on price and that extends to marketers and packers. It'll open us up so we'll be able to work more days. More area to work so we don't stress the bottom."

Jay took off his gloves, boots and weights, drank water, and emptied the compressor's tank.

"You know, they called at 9:00, and law didn't get here until 11:15," George said. "I'm glad the boat wasn't on fire."

"People just lost their heart—it's the end of the season and it's been a rough one. The culprits are parasites and toxins and what else."

As the *Night Moves* rounded Bennett Point, the landing came into view. The other workboats that had been there during the morning had never left. "People just lost their heart —it's the end of the season and it's been a rough one," George said. "And if you hadn't made what you're going to make by now you're in serious trouble."

"The culprits are the parasites and toxins and what else," he went on. "That's why we've had a rough year. Those hand tongers, they're just trying to find someone to blame."

It had been a rough year for oystermen all around the Bay, for hand tongers as well as divers, patent tongers as well as dredgers, all season long. Marylanders harvested less than a million bushels for the first time ever, not much compared to the recent average of two-and-a-half, nothing at all compared with Maryland's fifteen million bushel all-time-high harvest in 1885. But there was bright news, too. Two years of high spat sets promised better harvests in the years to come, if salinity stayed low, if disease kept at bay. And George placed great store in reports he had heard of recent improvements in water quality, of tertiary treatment plants that would dilute the Bay's waters rather than enrich them. And Maryland, Virginia and the District of Columbia had all finally banned phosphate detergents after years of haggling, and it seemed that farmers and others were making some attempt to keep nutrients out of the estuary.

As he pulled up to the bulkhead and began unloading his oysters, and looking for the marine police officer who would deliver his long-awaited citation, George seemed satisfied with the day, with his encounter with the marine police. "Well, I'm glad it's about over," he said, though it wasn't clear whether he meant his run-in with the law or the rough season just ending. He paused, then added, "Move on to something else now."

When he spoke, everything seemed in fact to move, the waves across the Wye, the light across the clouds. Early March, the pound netters would be driving their posts into the bottom of the Bay, the eels would be returning from the Sargasso Sea, guided by a compass undiscovered and inexplicable. And as the season turned, crab pots and trotlines would emerge from sheds where they overwintered, boats would get new caulking and engines new oil. As faithful as ospreys, people would return to the rivers, to the Bay, and a select few, some drawn by circumstance and some by conviction, would turn to the next cycle, following for another year the water trades.

WORKING THE CHESAPEAKE: WATERMEN ON THE BAY was designed by Sandy Harpe.
The text was composed in Goudy, the headlines in Weiss.
The papers are 70-pound Glatfelter Offset Text and 12-point Carolina Cover.
The book was printed, smythe sewn and bound by McNaughton & Gunn.
Twenty-six lettered copies have been cloth bound in Roxite
and signed by the author and the artist.